PROFILES
FOR SUCCESS

ABOUT THE AUTHOR

Distinguished Professor Richard F. Edlich was a Ford Foundation Scholar who gained early admission to Lafayette College at age 15. Three years later, he was accepted as an early admission student to New York University School of Medicine, where he received his M.D. He completed a general surgery residency at the University of Minnesota Health Sciences Center. During that time, he also received his Ph.D. He has taught at the University of Virginia since 1971, beginning as an instructor and becoming Distinguished Professor of Plastic Surgery and Professor of Biomedical Engineering.

During his years at Virginia, Dr. Edlich has served as director of the University of Virginia Burn Center, director of the Life Support Learning Center, and co-director of the Emergency Nurse Practitioner Training Program and the National Crisis Center for the Deaf. As director of the Emergency Medical Service of the University of Virginia Medical Center from 1973 until 1982, he was responsible for the coordination and implementation of a regional emergency system in Virginia that has received national recognition. A specialist in research on the biology of wound repair and infection, he has published seven books and more than 700 scientific articles and chapters on these subjects. His latest book, "Medicine's Deadly Dust," is a nationally acclaimed report documenting the life threatening dangers of powders on surgical and examination gloves.

As a teacher, Dr. Edlich is a popular speaker whose addresses are remembered by the University and professional societies. In 1985, he gave the Kennedy Lecture to the Society of Academic Emergency Medicine. In 1987 and 1992, the graduating class of medical students of the University of Virginia asked him to deliver its Baccalaureate address. He delivered the commencement address to the graduating nursing students in 1993. In recognition of his commitment to teaching, the University's Alumni Association honored Dr. Edlich with its Distinguished Professor Award. Dr. Edlich was the recipient of the Commonwealth of Virginia's Council of Higher Education's Outstanding Faculty Award in 1989. His work was honored by the Southeastern Society for Plastic Reconstructive Surgery's first prize for surgical research, the Virginia Surgical Society's Bigger-Lehman Award, and the University Association of Emergency Medicine's President's Award. A member of Alpha Omega Alpha and the Raven Society, he received the Hal Jayne Award from the Society for Academic Emergency Medicine for his academic excellence in 1989. In 1991, Dr. Edlich received the Thomas Jefferson Award, the highest academic honor presented by the University of Virginia. The Sigma Theta Tau International Beta Kappa Chapter presented him with its community service award in 1995. Lafayette College presented the George Washington Kidd Class of 1876 Award to Dr. Edlich for achieving distinction in his career in medicine and teaching.

Through the generous support of friends and colleagues, endowments were established for the annual Richard F. Edlich Burn Lecture, the Richard F. Edlich Chair in Plastic Surgical Research and the annual Richard F. Edlich Medical Student Research Award in Emergency Medicine.

PROFILES FOR SUCCESS

Lessons in Teaching, Healing, Curing and Living

Richard F. Edlich, MD, PhD

Distinguished Professor of Plastic Surgery and
Professor of Biomedical Engineering
University of Virginia Health Sciences Center

Published by
Vandamere Press
P.O. Box 5243
Arlington, VA 22205
USA

Copyright 1999
Vandamere Press

ISBN 0-918339-49-9

Manufactured in the United States of America. Designed and typeset in Ehrhardt MT
by Northeastern Graphic Services, Inc., Hackensack, New Jersey.

Acknowledgements

The trials and tribulations of childhood can have a profound influence on our lives. In some cases, they become a guide for our journeys through life. When I was 11 years old, my mother had abdominal surgery for a large ovarian cyst that resulted in adhesive stringlike bands resulting in recurrent episodes of intestinal obstruction. Her illness was one of my first *life-defining experiences* that caused me to leave home at age 15 in search of a cure for her illness. I received a Ford Foundation scholarship that allowed me early admission to Lafayette College. Three years later I further accelerated my educational program gaining entrance to New York University School of Medicine. One of the most important events in my life occurred after my first academic examination during my first year of medical school. After passing this test, my fellow medical students invited me to spend an exciting evening at the race track. Our victorious betting at Roosevelt Raceway garnered sufficient moneys to celebrate at a nightclub, the Piccolo Club, near the medical school. As I entered the club, I immediately noted a beautiful singer who sang love songs as if they came from Heaven. I was so taken by her presence that I was unable to speak to her. When I left the nightclub, I shared with my medical school colleagues that I planned to marry this singer, whose name I still did not know. This decision was the wisest one of my life. Carol Taylor became my beloved wife on May 6, 1961. Carol took a starring role in my life, as well as in the Broadway musical theatre. She starred on Broadway as Maria in Leonard Bernstein's classic musical, "West Side Story." During the last 37 years, Carol has been my best friend and advisor in our exciting life journey that is recounted in my book, *Profiles for Success*. Carol has sung magical songs on her companion CD to this book, "From Somewhere in My Heart" that best express the joy and beauty of our journey.

Carol Taylor Edlich

Carol and I have lived for more than 21 years in a two-story English country home nestled in 18 acres of pasture land. A blue heron still glides into the motionless waters of the Mirror Lake next to our home. Two does and three fawns eat the tall grass near our barn. Our beautiful children, Elizabeth Carol, Richard and Rachel Carol spent their adolescent years on this farm on which they raised horses, cattle, pigs, dogs, goats and cats. It was their Noah's Ark. Our farm provided a nurturing environment in which we would become best friends. Christmas trees lining our driveway provide wonderful holiday memories. While our children have left the nest pursuing their own quixotic journeys, they frequently return home for family celebrations that acknowledge the growth of our family. On September 3, 1995 Richard married Patricia Cooper in a ceremony on our farm. Elizabeth Carol exchanged vows with Dale Kinsella on our new checkerboard patio overlooking Mirror Lake on September 26, 1998. Their son, Matthew, is the newest addition to our family. As we fertilized the soil that allowed flowers and our children to grow around our home, Carol and I have opened up our hearts in the book and its companion CD to allow you a picture of our souls.

As I wrote *Profiles for Success*, I enlisted the wise help and advice of Art Brown, who published this book. Art is a visionary in the publishing world whose enormous talents attract the most gifted writers. His long time associate, Pat Berger, crafted the organizational structure of this book.

I remain deeply indebted to Tom Labrecque, the gifted leader, for writing the foreword for this book. The thoughtful introduction of John Keegan, the brilliant lawyer and foundation president, highlights how our plan for self-actualization can change the world. I must also acknowledge Tom Labrecque and John Keegan for their willingness to bring *Profiles for Success* to the attention of the news media and society.

The birth of this book was considerably facilitated by the editorial assistance of Brooke Carl, who has become a knowledgeable historian of my teachers and personal journey.

Foreword

For the past quarter century, I have had a first row-center view of the transformation of the financial services industry and in fact, American industry as a whole. I have watched globalization and with it, the rapid adoption of the free market economics around the world, industry consolidation, changing customer expectations, and of course, the accelerating pace of technological innovation challenge the very best companies including my own, Chase Manhattan. The firms that have flourished in the face of tremendous change- it seems to me-share several characteristics, including a commitment to innovation, flexibility, decisiveness and a passionate drive for results.

Business, of course, is hardly alone in this transformation. The sheer pervasiveness of change is reshaping the fabric and mission of our social and educational structures, and indeed, has become a profound influence on the course of individual lives.

But change in and of itself is neutral. It is how men and women respond and react to change that determines the outcome of events. I have watched companies and governments rise and fall and seen individuals challenge and rise from adversity to fulfill great, even noble causes. The capacity and personal fortitude to see opportunity in difficulty, move forward in the midst of crisis and uncertainty and maintain a level of passionate commitment: these are all characteristics of individuals who make a lasting mark on society even in the face of tremendous ongoing change.

The chapters that follow represent the thoughts of one such person- a truly unique and gifted man- a well trained scientist, doctor and teacher who has joined these skills with a sound philosophy of everyday human existence. It is this combination which makes Dick Edlich's proposals set forth in this book so interesting.

The material that you are about to share is in many ways an understanding of human partnerships. The partnership between:

    teacher and student;
    doctor and patient;
    the living and the dying;
    the privileged and those who are discriminated against.

Dick Edlich has been each of these at various times in his life, including feeling the discrimination associated with the disabilities of his illness, multiple sclerosis.

This book derives its uniqueness not only from Dick's mastering of each role listed above, but also his understanding that the paired roles are partnerships which, when fully understood, truly have the power to alter the outcomes in very positive ways. Having lived these roles, Dick is in the rare position of experiencing the emotions and thoughts of the scientist, teacher, student, doctor and patient, who has now brought them together into an integrated whole.

The consequences of these unusual life experiences is a thoughtful set of prescriptions which can help to transform positively society and the traditional ways we look at its medical and social problems. It is also an awakening which cries out for the leadership, accountability and involvement of us all.

Profiles for Success: Lessons in Teaching, Healing, Curing and Living gives us very practical and pragmatic solutions for a host of scientific, medical and societal issues, while showing us his inner self, and in the process, opening our own minds and broadening our understanding of human existence. We have responsibility to further contribute to this experience, building the accountable healthcare and educational systems so important to the future of our society.

Thomas G. Labrecque
President
The Chase Manhattan Corporation
New York, New York

Introduction

During the past year, Thomas Alva Edison was honored as "Man of the Millennium" by a special edition of *Life* magazine because he was recognized as the person who contributed most to benefiting human kind throughout the past 1000 years. Edison had no formal education. He came from no wealth. From early childhood, he was virtually deaf. Faced with his personal challenges, Edison was able to convert obstacles into opportunities. His inventions transformed our society, leaving a legacy deserved of this prestigious award. As a young man, Edison understood Dick Edlich's dynamic paradigm of being *present in the moment* when he began his invention journey. He conceived his first product, the vote counter, without seeking the wise counsel of the consumer. Because the consumer did not perceive an immediate need for his unique invention, revenues generated for the vote counter were very limited. For some novices, this disappointing response might have ended their careers. Undaunted by this defeat, Edison turned this crisis into an opportunity. He realized that he must be *present in the moment* with the consumer to determine their needs. When he appreciated the consumers' needs he would then devise products that responded to these perceived needs. He then enlisted the help of *powerful problem solvers* in his laboratory to assist him in creating new products. Edison invented the incandescent light bulb, the motion picture camera and the phonograph. The invention of the phonograph is especially notable because the deaf inventor created sounds for those who could hear. During his illustrious engineering career, he devised 1,093 patents which created a *societal transformation*. His inventions made the world a more enjoyable place to be.

Despite Edison's enormous contributions to humankind, Edison's legacy, which includes the Invention Factory in West Orange, New Jersey, was on the most endangered list of the National Trust for Historic

Preservation. Consequently, the Trustees of the Charles Edison Fund established the Thomas Alva Edison Preservation Foundation. Like Edison and Edlich, the Trustees were *present in the moment* to the legacy of Edison and were determined to convert a potential crisis into a national educational opportunity. We enlisted the help of *powerful problem solvers* in fundraising, marketing, engineering, science, academe, law, accounting and finance to achieve a common *goal*: empowerment of the Edison Legacy. We undertook an $80 million campaign to preserve the Edison Legacy by upgrading the seven national historic sites across the country and creating an endowment to preserve the Edison Papers, the largest collection of personal papers in the world besides those of Leonardo da Vinci. This effort, when completed, will create a *societal transformation* by establishing Edison as the role model for children entering the next century and millennium.

After citing personal examples of his own *life-defining experiences* which fit the above paradigm, Dick Edlich welcomes you to his Academic Village, a village of opportunities without barriers or walls that has an atmosphere friendly to learning. Traditional lines of hostility between teacher and student, like the grading system, are gone. All his students are honor students. The private sector is welcomed to share the experience. Teachers are students and students are teachers . He encourages, nay challenges, you to become his teacher. Do it! Wangensteen, his teacher and mentor, knows he was one "helluva" student. Enjoy the encounter.

The development of Lorenzo's oil by the Odones was proof to Edlich that the impossible is possible and the incurable is curable. He brings out the Jonas Salk and Don Quixote in all of us. Although oxymoronic, he is both a romantic and realist who ties the two together by unconditional love. "One never gets enough hugs," he argues. Although interested in novel ideas he, like Edison, seeks knowledge not as an end, in and of itself, but rather as a means to create new cures and products. His contributions to medicine include lifesaving products and drugs for the treatment of burns and accidental wound injuries. For the Commonwealth of Virginia, he championed the development of a modern emergency medical system that has saved thousands of lives. Edison would be proud of what he did with the help of Reverend Jerry Falwell in establishing the National Emergency Medical Telecommunications System for the Deaf. How often the case has been that success follows not in spite of a handicap, but because of one. Edison was deaf. Edlich has multiple sclerosis (MS).

As teacher, student, gadfly, physician, scientist, physician-as-patient, motivator and challenger, Edlich is a man of no small moment. He thinks big! He deserves a national platform from which to launch a $250 million campaign to cure MS. He thinks right! In general, we need more federal funding for medical research and, in particular, for chronic diseases, like MS. The $2 billion spent annually to care for MS patients is staggering. Edlich warns us that the cost of caring for chronic illness may bankrupt society. Let us help him find the cures.

With Wangensteen as teacher, Elisabeth Kübler-Ross as advisor who helped him embrace the gifts of life and Carol, best friend and wife, translating this wonderful book to music in her superb CD, "From Somewhere in My Heart," his life and message become the focal point of the Academic Village classroom in and from which we all learn.

And make no mistake about it, his *life-defining experiences* support his willingness to stand and fight, especially if the cause is both right and worthwhile. He is not afraid to "rock the boat" and, once rocked, to take the helm with his colleagues and right the course. Our good friends, Beth and Charles Ross, are very proud to be partners in his journey.

If you want to make your life count, make a difference, be motivated, inspired, challenged, strive to perfect your inner spirit and are not a "Doubting Thomas," read this book. If none of these things interest you, read it anyway and see how the other half lives. Enjoy the journey.

Back to Edison and Edlich. Both are visionaries. Both are doers. In his life and *Profiles for Success*, Edlich constructs a powerful paradigm of solving problems with which humanity is both confronted and afflicted. Edison said, "There is a better way to do it. Find it." Dick Edlich did just that.

John P. Keegan
Chair and President
Charles Edison Fund
Thomas Alva Edison Preservation Foundation
East Orange, New Jersey

Contents

PROFILES
FOR SUCCESS

1

My Invitation

Profiles for Success is an invitation to teach yourself and others to live a self-actualized and empowered life and transform the culture of our society from emotions of fear to those of love. In the process, you may heal the sick and injured, cure incurable illnesses or achieve personal *goals* that you will set for yourself. I am writing this book for each of you because I believe that you have a burning desire to find meaning for your life. I think that you perceive a dualism to your life in which you want to be part of a winning team and, at the same time, be a star in your own right. In other words, you want your life to count. When you have achieved your *goal*, your life will become significant to you, as well as to society. For many of us, our missions in life are misdirected, ineffective, inefficient and unproductive. My thesis is that we have a choice to find new ways to self-actualize and transform our lives and work together to change the world.

I have transformed my life by applying lessons learned from seven gifted individuals who made dramatic improvements in our world. I will describe to you the life journeys of one renowned teacher, three healers, two curers and one spiritual guide so that you will understand more clearly their profiles for success. I have examined their personal odysseys carefully in an effort to share with you how they were able to achieve their dreams. I have identified common thematic experiences in their lives as well as many comparable personal responses to these *life-defining experiences.* I believe that their similar experiences and responses indicate that their lives can be lessons to us all in achieving our own self-actualization. My associations with each of them have been reminiscent of that of a mountain climber who nears the peak of a mountain. Their teachings have changed my vision of myself and the world and presented new opportunities for me to be a partner in *societal transformation.* I anticipate that their life experiences and personal responses will have a similar positive impact on your life, allowing you to achieve your destiny.

First, each of these individuals had a *life-defining experience* that was viewed as a crisis. These *life-defining experiences* immediately caught their attention because they involved emotional and physical pain, suffering, and death and dying. Each of these individuals used four similar adaptive or healthy coping strategies to these *life-defining experiences* that allowed them to remain focused on the problem: (1) presence in the moment, (2) goal setting, (3) recruitment of powerful problem solvers, and (4) societal transformation.

They did not go the route of fright-or-flight, nor the route of helplessness when confronting these challenging problems; rather, each of these individuals was *present in the moment* to these *life-defining experiences* that involved the suffering and pain of the diseased or injured person. Being *present in the moment* is a unique process of nonjudgmental awareness that allows you to see more clearly into the minds of others as well as into your own mind. Many miss these moments because they allow their minds to be distracted by unrelated occurrences. When you are *present in the moment*, your mind acts like a lens, taking the scattered and reactive thoughts of your mind and focusing them into a coherent source of thoughts about living, problem-solving and healing. As they were *present in the moment*, they all displayed unconditional love for others. Fear was not part of their vocabulary. While they interacted with others, all assumed some responsibility for the afflicted and grieved for the losses of loved ones and families. Moreover, they all recognized the societal implications of this *life-defining experience*, realizing that thousands of other people were suffering from the same affliction. Each tried intellectually to understand the scientific cause of the life-threatening illness or injury. Their emotional reactions must be viewed as courageous because many members of society, faced with these same losses, would distance themselves from the afflicted to lessen their personal pain. Some individuals become immobilized with fear and believe they cannot tolerate the pain. Others respond by ignoring the existence of this calamity, hoping that it will not happen to them. This personal distancing usually ends any scientific discovery of the mechanism of disease or injury, often by attributing the crisis to an act of God.

Second, each individual was a brave soul who had the unique ability to convert a *crisis into an opportunity*. Their adventure began by identifying a clear understandable *goal* that was empowering to them as well as other individuals. *Goal-setting* was an essential component of their successful achievements. Their definition of their *goals* became synonymous with their life mission statements. Their *goals* touched the hearts of every human being. Remember the defining words of the world-renowned trauma surgeon, Dr. R Adams Cowley, "I want to save the lives of injured Americans." Setting such well-defined *goals* is frightening to most of us for many reasons that usually relate to personal doubts about ourselves. Do you have the intellectual capability, the leadership skills, and the physical endurance to tackle gigantic problems? The answers to each of these questions by these leaders was a resounding, YES! Their journeys began with gathering information from the scientific literature and from associates about the speculated cause of the crisis. Then, the individual began a search for other injured or ill patients who had experienced similar crises. They became consumed with the individual's problem and tried personally to devise plans to identify the cause, treatment or cure of the crisis.

Third, each individual identified and enrolled *powerful problem-solvers*, realizing that they could not solve the problem without the help of other individuals. They met with gifted individuals and tried to devise problem-solving plans. They attended what seemed to be endless meetings that focused on finding sufficient moneys to support pilot research projects that examined the mechanism and treatment of this disease or injury. On the basis of these comprehensive research studies, these teams of passionate individuals tested their scientific hypotheses. Once a speculated treatment or cure was devised, this team tested the validity of this treatment with a clinical trial. Ultimately, these teams of *powerful problem-solvers* would find a cure or treatment of the disease or injury in another afflicted individual.

Finally, armed with one or two successful treatments of these crises, these teams of *powerful problem-solvers* had to enact a *societal transformation program* that would benefit all individuals with these diseases or injuries. Moreover, they would have to discuss the scientific merits of the new and promising therapeutic approaches. Ultimately, they would have to enlist the help of medical and political leaders who would enact legislation, raise sufficient funds and teach the public about this now preventable crisis. They challenged the dissenters against change by debating the issues, rather than defaming the dissenter. As these teams of *powerful problem-solvers* successfully enacted *societal transformation*, these gifted individuals graciously acknowledged their colleagues and friends who participated in this successful journey. The essence of this team of *powerful problem-solvers* vibrated with their intimate connection with their colleagues.

My personal transformation evolved through my connection with these unique individuals whose professional contributions revolutionized teaching, healthcare, science and, quite simply, the process of living. Their successes are due to the remarkable clarity of their vision and those dreams they dared to achieve. Working in environments in which their visions were castigated or suppressed by colleagues, well-intentioned or not, they worked tirelessly and provided irrefutable evidence of the merits of their revolutionary ideas. Finally, and most importantly, they devised a sound forum in which their dreams could evolve into reality. Their revolutionary concepts lend credence to our inherent belief that we can accomplish our individual dreams and, in so doing, affect *societal transformation*.

Dr. Owen Wangensteen identified his *life-defining experience* shortly after he became Professor and Chairman of the Department of Surgery at the University of Minnesota in 1930. He was at that time called on to care for patients with obstruction of the intestines. The only effective method of treatment of the blocked intestines was surgery that usually had devastating life-threatening consequences with an operative mortality rate of 60%. Because 80% of the patients who suffered from obstruction had undergone previous abdominal surgery, Dr. Wangensteen knew these patients well. He was often the surgeon at the initial operative procedure and later for the treatment of the life-threatening intestinal obstruction. Because of Dr. Wangensteen's long friendships with his patients, he assumed considerable responsibility for the patients' deaths. Dr. Wangensteen's personal numbing guilt became a catalyst for his developing a nonoperative management of intestinal obstruction. His treatment dramatically reduced the mortality rate of treatment of patients with intestinal obstruction to 6%. When he devised his successful treatment, he enlisted the help of medical students, surgical residents, basic scientists and surgical faculty. Their victory was an announcement to his surgical training program as well as the world that miracles could occur in Minnesota. Dr. Wangensteen devised an educational system for pioneering surgeons whose research dramatically changed healthcare. Dr. C. Walton Lillehei, one of his most gifted protégés, performed some of the first successful operations on the human heart that laid the framework for the field of cardiothoracic surgery. The merit of Dr. Wangensteen's educational approach was questioned from its inception, and he was asked to resign his position shortly after appointment. He remained at the same university during his entire academic career, training more teachers in surgery than anyone in the last century. Lessons I learned during my eight years of surgical residency with Dr. Wangensteen allowed me in later years to form a multidisciplinary team of gifted scientists. These scientists devised innovative treatments and products that are being used in our new 16-bed burn and wound-healing center at the University of Virginia Health Sciences Center, which is recognized throughout the world.

Jim Mills, R A. Cowley and David Boyd were pioneers in emergency medical care who knew exactly the essential components of a comprehensive emergency medical system. Jim Mills and R A. Cowley had *life-defining experiences* during their military service to our country in World War II. They witnessed heroic lifesaving emergency care orchestrated by a team of well-trained military personnel. They knew that injured soldiers would receive better care on the battlefield than on the streets of our nation's capital, Washington, D.C. When they returned to civilian life, they had the agonizing realization that civilians with life-threatening injuries and illnesses were dying unnecessarily in our country with its antiquated emergency medical systems. David Boyd had his *life-defining experience* working in R A. Cowley's embryonic trauma unit at the University of Maryland. David was sickened to find out that many of the trauma beds lay empty because physicians in Maryland were reluctant to send their patients to Cowley for his lifesaving treatments. Mills became the leading force for identifying a new role for physicians in emergency medicine and devising an educational training program that allowed for the certification of emergency physicians. Cowley complemented Mills' efforts by designing and developing the first trauma center equipped with a multidisciplinary staff prepared to save the accident victim's life. Realizing that emergency services had to work as a coordinated system of care, Boyd conceptualized and implemented the Federal Emergency Medical Systems Act. The Act facilitated the development of coordinated emergency medical services throughout the country and ensured that all people would have access to emergency medical care. The sociological permutations of this concept of "equal care" were dramatic. In the emergency departments, the violence that has become so prevalent in our society stood out bleakly under the bright lights as the injured and victimized flooded in for care. Not only did these three medical innovators leave as their legacy the trained, certified emergency physician, certified trauma centers and organized emergency services in each state, they also promoted the need for sensitivity in the medical community to the often tragic plights of their patients and created a forum in which the abuse and addictions inherent in our society could no longer be ignored. These pioneers in healthcare taught me the strategies that allowed me to implement a model statewide emergency medical system for Virginia that has saved thousands of lives. This system has dramatically changed healthcare at the University of Virginia Health Sciences Center with our development of a new trauma center, a Department of Emergency Medicine with a residency training program, a regional poison control center, a crisis center staffed with a psychiatrist and social worker, a microvascular surgery center and an emergency aircraft evacuation system.

Michaela and Augusto Odone have left as their legacy to society an inspirational story of family empowerment. Faced with the life-threatening inherited illness of their beloved son, Lorenzo, this husband and wife without medical credentials had a unified, clear vision of their *goal*: "cure our son." Despite the eloquent opposition of doctors and charities, they gathered a team of talented scientists who devised and implemented a cure for this genetic disease. Realizing that Lorenzo's advanced condition was not cured by their diet therapy, they have committed themselves to restoring his injured brain using this same empowered approach toward scientific discovery. When I developed multiple sclerosis (MS), I recognized the unique social isolation facing physicians who become patients. The Odones taught me that the ultimate outcome of my illness would be determined by the innovative partnerships I would develop with compassionate scientists and physicians. Spurred on by the support of other patients with MS, I have developed a modern rehabilitation program for patients with MS that is used throughout the world. I have enrolled a talented team of scientists who have developed a rational and valid approach to cure my illness.

For Elisabeth Kübler-Ross, her *life-defining experience* was her conversations with dying patients that provided her with a prescription for living. Entering the field of psychiatry at a time when the subject of death and dying was still taboo, Elisabeth Kübler-Ross began an internationally recognized dialogue with dying patients that allowed her to identify the different psychological stages that accompany death. The publication of her landmark book, *On Death and Dying*[1], caused her to be banished from academic medicine. She transformed her dismissal from the University of Chicago into an opportunity for her to understand the potential self-actualization of the human race with her workshops on life, death and transition. Her workshops healed the wounds of the emotionally, physically and sexually abused and provided a medium in which the oppressed found their voice and power. The development of hospices throughout our country was a direct result of her contributions to the care of the terminally ill. This development is viewed justifiably as a revolutionary advance in medicine. She transformed my life as I attended her workshops and served on the board of her retreat center. She devised for me a prescription that allowed me to truly live instead of merely exist.

My exciting personal and professional adventures with these leaders have been a transforming experience. Their teachings allowed me to perceive new horizons filled with many, new unanswered questions. In the following chapters, I will share with you the *profiles for success* of these dreamers that have transformed teaching, healthcare, science and our lives. After I have recounted their courageous journeys, I have related my personal odyssey that exemplifies their profound impact on my life. On the basis of lessons learned from their experiences, I have compiled prescriptions for teaching, healing, curing, and living. The adventures of these leaders are so filled with excitement, bravery and struggle that they have served as a continued source of inspiration and hope for my life as I work to achieve my own visions. I have written this book with the hope that these prescriptions will resonate with you.

The concept of challenge and conflict in the face of an unbending society is by no means a new one. The struggles of my teachers often remind me of the story told in Miguel de Cervantes de Saavedra's tale *Don Quixote de la Mancha*[2], the most widely recognized book in Spanish literature. In the story, Don Quixote and his trusty servant, Sancho Panza, take the road on a campaign to restore the age of chivalry, battling evil. In the novel's most memorable adventure, they ride through a countryside dotted with dozens of windmills. Don Quixote, covered with shield and lance at ready, spurs his horse forward and drives his weapon into the revolving sail of the first windmill. He is hurled to the ground and his lance broken. The combat is replete with symbols. The windmills can represent the suspicious surgical teachers who conspired to end the career of surgery's greatest teacher, the reluctant medical community unwilling to transfer dying patients to the trauma centers, the charities and physicians who will not listen to their benefactors or society's fear of death that attempts to silence a Swiss psychiatrist. Regardless of the symbolism, the greater message is clear: only a positive act of will is capable of attacking anything; success or failure is unimportant. The clarity of Don Quixote's vision is further exemplified when he encounters two prostitutes whom he perceives as ladies of quality. They respond kindly to his courteous greeting and appear to transform their outward identities to agree with his ideal image. This tale is consistent with the psychological truism: if one anticipates superior performance from another, one will receive the expected. The reverse, of course, is also true.

So powerful is Don Quixote's legacy that we have created in our language a word that defines his vision: quixotism. It is defined as the universal quality characteristic of any visionary action. Our quixotic spirit must relentlessly pursue our dreams that will ultimately transform society and our identity. Often held up to ridicule, frequently embarrassed, quixotic individuals must pursue dreams that will allow them to inherit a place in history.

I have summarized action plans for your life as easily memorable prescriptions. You will soon find out that you can master these seemingly unachievable *goals*. To achieve your impossible dreams, follow this two-point plan:

1. After reading the chapters, reflect carefully on each prescription so that you can incorporate these principles into your life. Make a photocopy of each prescription and place it in a site where you will see it every day. As these principles become ingrained in your subconsciousness, they will become integrated into your life.
2. Set deadlines for incorporating these prescriptions into your life.

I am convinced that these prescriptions can change your lives. They are applicable to a wide variety of settings that include you, your family, school, hospital, government agency and church or any setting in which people work together. I am here to support your transformation, acknowledge your successes, as well as disappointments, by e-mail at profiles@cstone.net. I will join you on your quest as you will ultimately become my teacher. If these prescriptions can empower you to be quixotic, to awaken your imagination and strength of will, then I have achieved my quest.

2

Teacher's Mission

"It is my conviction that great teachers focus as importantly upon the unknown as the known. Our disciplines advance solely by pushing back the topography of ignorance. When the challenge of the unknown captures the professor's students, the teacher's mission is fulfilled."

Dr. Owen H. Wangensteen

Since 1973, I have been a *teacher* at the University of Virginia. The University has faithfully supported my academic career by establishing an endowed chair in 1980 for my faculty position that provided a generous annual salary. This endowed chair silenced any personal consideration of a more lucrative career in private practice. A recipient for an endowed chair is selected on evidence of productive scholarship and effective teaching. The privilege of teaching students as well as faculty remains the primary impetus for continuing my career in higher education. My performance and success as a teacher have been recognized and celebrated by the University community. In 1986, I was selected for the Outstanding Teacher Award by the Alumni Association. I received the Outstanding Teacher Award from the Council of Higher Education of the Commonwealth of Virginia in 1989. The recipients of this latter award are selected from the 12,000 faculty of the 105 state-supported institutions and 2,500 faculty members of the 55 private institutions in Virginia. Governor Gerald L. Baliles presented me with a sculpture by the talented artist, Kent F. Ipsen, Professor of Art at the Virginia Commonwealth University. Appropriately, his sculpture has a trefoil configuration that celebrates the partnership among teaching, business and government. After learning of my awards for teaching, students as well as faculty frequently ask me to identify the ideal characteristics of a teacher.

Dr. Owen H. Wangensteen, my mentor, recognized as the greatest teacher of surgery in this century.

My philosophy regarding teaching has been formulated primarily by my close personal relationship with my beloved mentor, Dr. Owen Wangensteen, Professor and Chairman of the Department of Surgery at the University of Minnesota, who is recognized as the greatest teacher of surgery during this century. Dr. Wangensteen signed most of his correspondence with his initials, OHW. He was esteemed and loved by the students, residents and colleagues who referred to him as "Dr. Wangensteen," "the Chief," or "the Professor." Because of our admiration, esteem and respect for him, he was never called by his first name, Owen. While cumbersome in my reflections of him, I will continue to refer to him as Dr. Wangensteen.

To understand his approach to teaching, I must further acquaint you with him. He was born at Lake Park, Minnesota, where his father, an immigrant from Norway, was a merchant and farmer.[1] Dr. Wangensteen grew up on his father's farm. He helped to care for horses, cows and pigs. A herd of 50 pregnant sows on his father's farm was unable to give birth to their young, causing the local veterinarian to recommend that they be sent to slaughter. After two sows were put to death because they couldn't deliver, the young farmer succeeded in delivering a litter of live piglets from the third sow by using his hand to assist delivery. During the next three weeks, he delivered more than 300 piglets in the same manner. This effort caused this young man to drop out of school for three weeks. Dr. Wangensteen later commented that, "Those of you who have had obstetrical experience know such assignments are time-consuming, especially for multiple births. I can still feel after many years the warmth of my father's sense of pride in the accomplishment." This success convinced his father that his son should study medicine. His father's wish for him to become a doctor was to be fulfilled. His father died owning land, but having no money. At the time of his father's death, Dr. Wangensteen was a surgical fellow making $600 a year (room and board not included), and his older brother practiced law in Minnesota. Dr. Wangensteen commented that he and his older brother ". . . had to help put our younger brother and sister through college so we did experience some rather difficult times."

By 1930, he had become Chairman of the Department of Surgery of the University of Minnesota Health Sciences Center, a position he held for 37½-years. He transformed the University of Minnesota into a great center for surgery and attracted a group of brilliant young surgeons to do research on impossible problems. His lifelong recognition of the relevance of basic science and the insight to be derived from research in the training of young surgeons created the milieu and opportunities for great surgical achievements. During the period of almost 40 years in which he served as Chairman of the Department of Surgery, he became the greatest surgical educator of the 20th century. The future academic careers for his residents were indeed impressive. Thirty-eight became department chairs; 31 accepted positions as division heads of their departments; 72 were directors of training programs; 110 became full professors; and 18 had appointments as associate professors. Only 14 individuals started their academic careers as full-time faculty members and left teaching for private practice. It is important to enumerate the breadth of the pioneering research accomplishments of Wangensteen and his students that revolutionized medicine. In this favorable environment uncluttered by the cobwebs of tradition, significant developments in surgery were forthcoming: open heart surgery; the heart–lung machine; cardiac pacemaker; conservative management of intestinal obstruction; heart, pancreatic and intestinal transplantation; and metabolic surgery for weight loss as well as elevated blood cholesterol.

Dr. Wangensteen considered himself a "plumber of the intestinal tract," having worked clinically at both ends. One of his most notable innovations in medicine was his study of intestinal obstruction, which resulted in revolutionary clinical advances. His investigations defined the criteria for early diagnosis of intestinal obstruction and resulted in a remarkable approach to the management of this challenging clinical problem.

When Dr. Wangensteen became Chairman of Surgery of the University of Minnesota School of Medicine, he was frequently called on to care for patients with obstruction of the intestines. At that time, the only effective method of treatment of the blocked intestines was surgery. Without operations, patients with intestinal obstructions would almost invariably die. When surgery was performed to relieve intestinal obstructions, it was achieved by dividing the stringlike bands (adhesions) that compressed the intestines causing the obstruction. In addition, the surgeon would create an opening from the intestine to the exterior to drain the intestines above the obstruction (enterostomy). In the 1920s, almost half of the patients operated on for intestinal obstruction died!

About 80% of the patients who suffered from acute obstruction of the small intestines had undergone previous abdominal surgery that resulted in adhesive bands. In the great majority of patients, intestinal obstruction occurred as a complication of an earlier operation. Consequently, as the number of surgical operations increased rapidly with advances in medical technology, the number of patients with acute intestinal obstruction grew. Patients with acute intestinal obstructions burdened the hearts of most surgeons. After performing a successful abdominal surgical operation on their patients, the surgeons were shocked that these same patients later developed a potentially life-threatening intestinal obstruction. When they undertook emergency surgery to relieve the obstruction, most patients died. Their deaths were extremely troubling to surgeons because many had developed close friendships with these patients that began at the time of the first abdominal surgical operation. The patients as well as the surgeons generously credited the success of the first operation to the talented skills of the surgeon. The patients' accolades to the surgeon often was an ego–inflating experience. When the patient returned with a life-threatening intestinal obstruction months to years after the first procedure, it was a sad event for both the surgeon and patient because of the warm personal friendship that had developed. Heroic efforts to treat the obstructed intestine by surgical intervention usually resulted in the patient's death. With considerable sadness, many surgeons assumed some responsibility for the patient's death, causing them to be *present in the moment* with their patients and family. When Dr. Wangensteen accepted this responsibility for the death of his beloved patients with intestinal obstructions, the patients' deaths became his *life-defining experience*.

Dr. Wangensteen's personal numbing guilt about the patient's death became a catalyst for numerous scientific studies aimed at improving the management of patients with acute intestinal obstruction. His investigative studies changed his vision of intestinal obstruction from a catastrophe to *a life-transforming opportunity*. He identified a clear goal for his scientific journey: save the lives of patients with intestinal obstruction. To this end, he enrolled the help of medical students, surgical residents and surgical faculty who became *powerful problem-solvers*. Dr. Wangensteen and his beloved colleagues were among the first to establish that the gaseous distension in the obstructed intestines was largely caused by swallowed air. Sometime during 1931, Dr. Wangensteen postulated that, if the chief value of surgical enterostomy was to relieve the distension of the obstructed intestines by gas that consisted mostly of swallowed air, it might be possible to intercept the swallowed air in the stomach before it entered the intestines. Any gas already in the intestines could then dissipate gradually by absorption into the circulating blood. Late in the summer of 1931, he had the opportunity to test his hypothesis.

A 72-year-old gravely ill woman was admitted to the hospital suffering from intestinal obstruction of 72-hour duration. It was believed that if a lessening of distension could be accomplished, the risk of operation could be definitely decreased. After passage of a tube through her nose down through her esophagus into her stomach, Dr. Wangensteen attached a suction device to the tube to remove swallowed air and fluid in the stomach. The cramping pain, of which the patient complained, ceased immediately. After 40 hours of nasal gastric suction, there was a complete disappearance of gaseous distension. Because it was believed that she had a complete obstruction of her large bowel, an operation was performed to relieve the obstruction and the patient convalesced uneventfully. By 1932, the torrent of research that Dr. Wangensteen had done in collaboration with fellows and medical students had brought him to a revolutionary development in abdominal surgery. He had discovered that suction through a nasal gastric tube could relieve distention as effectively as surgical decompression. In July 1935, Dr. Wangensteen received the Samuel D. Gross prize from the Philadelphia Academy of Surgery, one of the highest honors given to American surgeons. The most satisfactory evidence of the value of Dr. Wangensteen's work came from the records of the Massachusetts General Hospital, where for the decade spanning 1928–1937, the mortality for patients treated for intestinal obstruction declined to 20%, less than half the mortality rate of 44% for the preceding decade, 1917–1928. It was the first real decline in death in intestinal obstruction for the 40-year period for which the hospital possessed statistics. Dr. Wangensteen's team of dedicated surgical scientists had successfully completed a *societal transformation program* in which its conservative management of intestinal obstruction was now benefiting patients with intestinal obstruction throughout the world. His pioneering successful treatment of intestinal obstruction had considerable impact on the educational culture of his surgical department. His surgical treatment program based on comprehensive well-controlled scientific studies emphasized that multidisciplinary research programs were necessary to solve complex surgical problems. Moreover, it reminded each faculty member that all surgical problems could be solved, causing hope to spring eternally in his department.

Dr. Wangensteen pointed out that, "The only complaint that patients on whom prolonged nasal gastric suction is being used is the sticky feeling or the soreness of the throat caused by the tube." He commented that, "The patient who may be inclined at first to swear at the tube, later swears by it." In January 1951, Ogden Nash[1] commented about Dr. Wangensteen's contributions to surgery. "May I find my final rest in Owen Wangensteen's intestine knowing that his masterly suction will assure my resurrection."

Dr. Wangensteen had considerable success in translating lessons learned in the care of patients with intestinal obstruction into a plan to prevent their illness. Because a previous abdominal surgical procedure anteceded the development of adhesions, Dr. Wangensteen believed that certain well-known technical factors played important roles. Dr. Wangensteen was especially concerned about the powder on surgeons' gloves that predisposed to adhesion formation. Dr. Wangensteen warned the medical community about the danger of surgical glove powders and stressed the importance of its removal from surgical gloves. "It is very important, therefore, that all participants of an operation observe the precaution of washing away carefully the trace of starch powder remaining on the outside of rubber gloves before starting the operation." Dr. Wangensteen longed for a time when surgical glove manufacturers could manufacture gloves without these dangerous powders that cause the adhesive bands that obstructed the intestines.

In my frequent meetings with Dr. Wangensteen, he often cautioned me that the road toward *success* can be a torturous and dangerous pathway.[3] He indicated that opposition would arise that would provide eloquent and disarming reasons for my abandoning my dreams. Smiling, he would remind me that the magnitude of the opposition would often be proportionate to the merits of the *goals*. He warned me that the zeal of my opponents might be sufficient to kill the messenger, rather than the message.

He shared with me an early experience in his career as Chairman of the Department of Surgery that almost led to his dismissal. Dr. Wangensteen had inherited a surgical staff consisting of only one full-time faculty member, a large number of able part-time surgeons and only one surgical resident. He indicated that one of his first academic *goals* was to enlarge his residency training program. He planned to support the young residents by ending the financial support for his part-time faculty and transferring these funds to support residency training. This termination of funding for the part-time faculty caused them to seek Dr. Wangensteen's dismissal as Chairman of the Department of Surgery. He recounted, "My professional neck, I can tell you now, lay extended upon the block for longer than I like to recall, while I waited hopefully for signs of help from friends whose support really counted. Ah, bless the memory of great and true friends! Dean Lyon, one of the greatest of the fine deans this medical school has had, Lotus Delta Coffman, president of the university, and William C. Mayo, distinguished regent of the university, and my own surgical teacher, Arthur C. Strachauer – these were men who came to my rescue. Where could one have found better or more effectual support? Consequently, as I think back on these events, I must confess that the stay of sentences and the confidence which my friends and colleagues then expressed in me was undoubtedly a strong, impelling force which has driven me on to strive to merit the kindly judgments and assurances I then received. Dick, when your professional neck lays extended upon the block, ask your friends for help."

His role as the consummate physician was inextricably linked to his mission as a teacher. He displayed five unique characteristics that accounted for his success as a teacher of surgery and which he instilled in all his students:[2]

- He was a *visionary* who realized that the secrets of illnesses could be uncovered by interdisciplinary research programs involving surgical residents and basic scientists.
- He was an articulate *leader* who was able to enroll talented surgeons to be involved in his mission, training teachers of surgery.
- He was a skilled *manager* who designed an eight-year educational program for his surgical residents that included two-year graduate training in research for a doctoral degree (Ph.D.) and a six-year clinical residency training program.
- He was a keen *listener* who had an uncanny ability to identify future leaders in surgery who would revolutionize healthcare.
- He was an innovative *fund-raiser* who viewed the doctor-patient relationship as a partnership in a journey through uncharted waters resulting in lifelong friendships in which his patients became the generous benefactors of his training program.

The three principles behind Dr. Wangensteen's educational system that accounted for his success as an educator are described below.

Develop an educational curriculum that is specifically designed to achieve the goal of training teachers of surgery.

Dr. Wangensteen's program of postgraduate training in surgery was created and refined by him over a period of 37 years of his administration. He realized that a multidisciplinary research experience was a prerequisite for his educational program. He stated, ". . . I felt strongly that the laboratory offered the best opportunity to provide the operative skills so essential in clinical surgery and that it was the only means by which the discipline of surgery could be advanced. Despite the restrictive influence of the long and trying years of the Depression (1929–1941), means were found to provide young surgeons pointing toward an academic career, with an opportunity to gain experience in physiological techniques in well-known laboratories."

As Dr. Wangensteen reflected on his educational program, he provided a narrative description of its curriculum: "In a sense, it has not been too difficult in our medical school to enlist the interest of young surgeons in research, inasmuch as every surgical fellow is required to register in the Graduate School and to work toward a graduate degree. I can still remember what a tremendous handicap I believed this requirement to be when I entered the surgical residency training program. Later, when I met men of my own age at meetings, where other residency plans of training were in vogue, I found it difficult to explain to them the advantages of our plan. As the years have gone by, however, it has become quite clear that it is an enormous advantage to have this hurdle in our midst. In my own instincts, had it not been for this exposure to research which made it necessary to struggle with an experimental project, I probably would never have learned how exciting research would be."

Because each of his residents had to be accepted by the Graduate School as a candidate for either a Masters or Doctorate degree, we had to complete research investigations for a graduate thesis as well as the required academic courses. This educational requirement was obviously complemented by comprehensive surgical clinical training experience needed for board certification in general surgery. During his 40 years as chairman, 138 residents were awarded doctorate degrees. This achievement also had other benefits to the residents' pursuit of an academic career as they used the research compiled for their theses in articles submitted to medical journals. Most residents upon graduating had already published a sufficient number of articles to ensure appointment and subsequent promotion to a tenured position in an academic department of surgery. Furthermore, the comprehensive nature of the research program allowed the graduates to be far more competitive than their peers in applying for federally funded research grants. After appointment to an academic position in a surgery department, most of his students sailed rapidly through the tenure process. I was promoted to the position of Full Professor in the Department of Plastic Surgery three years after joining the department. The average period of time after which a faculty member will receive tenure at the University of Virginia is seven years.

Dr. Wangensteen realized that his eight-year residency was a torturous and long adventure in which he would have to nurture and encourage his budding scientists. "Students who fail to get beyond the spoon-feeding phase remain in the nursery stage of development and never attain mature growth. The student with a good appetite for knowledge soon learns that the occasional feeding by his teacher does not appease his hunger. He learns how to feed himself. Moreover, the earnest student's conflict with unsettled problems drives him on and soon he is consumed with a desire to try to add a few tidbits to the stores upon which he has been drawing so generously in his formative years. In the beginning, he probably sallies forth in the spirit of adventure like a boy starting out on bright spring morning for an outing in the country. It is only a diversionary amusement for a day, then back to the old routine. But the attractions of research frequently prove far more fascinating than the student had dreamed; he will stay another day to enjoy the promising prospects of the outing. Days and weeks go by and when the student returns from his adventure, his outlook on life has changed. What he undertook as momentary recreation has now become an absorbing interest in his life."

Raise sufficient financial support to allow the educational program to succeed.

His educational program required considerable funds, which were not available in the days prior to the end of World War II. Consequently, Dr. Wangensteen continually searched for funds to support his training program. He found that his grateful patients wanted to express their gratitude to him by generously contributing financial support. Dr. Wangensteen often mentioned that he had developed a unique strategy to enroll his patients as donors to his growing program.

"When I began in the 1930s to attract a few private patients, I decided it unwise to present an affluent patient with a fee for service. It was a device that paid off handsomely for my department and the medical school. Let me tell you of one instance. There was a large woman who had cancer of the upper third of the rectum and had been advised by the best talent in the state to accept a colostomy. Her dear husband, who I came to know well, loved every milligram of her large frame. It proved to be feasible to preserve sphincteric function and to restore intestinal continuity. Ten years went by. Then, unannounced, the grateful husband came to my office with a friend. After 20 minutes of conversation, said the friend: 'Tell me, why are we here?' Said my friend: 'We are here to talk about your problem.' Retorted the visitor: 'I have no problem.' 'Yes, you have,' said my friend. 'It is your money. Your money is your problem and you must be generous to worthy causes.' The upshot was he telephoned me later in the day to say that our surprised visitor was contributing $100,000 for research. In fact, before he died, the visitor, convinced of the importance of research, contributed more than $400,000 to the Department of Surgery to support an aggressive research program."

During the weeks before Christmas, Dr. Wangensteen would schedule a fund-raising luncheon in the Faculty Club to which he invited potential donors. He would arrange the table seating so that the donors were always positioned next to a surgical faculty or resident staff. During the luncheon, the faculty and residents would update the donors on the success of their research efforts and acknowledge the donors for their contributions. A keynote address by one of his accomplished faculty, like Dr. Lillehei, would bring tears to the eyes of the donors, many of whose lives were saved by his miraculous surgical innovation. This intimate contact between the young investigators and interested audience brought literally millions of dollars to support his educational program.

He also realized that financial support must extend beyond the confines of his training program. Christiaan Bernard came to Minnesota from Cape Town, South Africa. Bernard had previously worked largely on problems relating to the bowel. He was one of the first to show experimentally that, if a segment of bowel was deprived of its blood supply during embryonic life, a narrowing of the intestine would follow that would result in obstruction. He came to Minnesota intending to extend his observations and spend some time in the experimental laboratory working on similarly related problems. He was soon fascinated with developments in intracardiac surgery in C. Walton Lillehei's laboratory. When he completed his training in Minnesota, Dr. Wangensteen helped him secure a substantial research grant that allowed him to initiate research studies in cardiac transplantation in South Africa. These experimental studies allowed him to successfully perform the first cardiac transplantation in a human being.

When I left Minnesota in 1971, Dr. Wangensteen arranged for adequate financial support that would allow me to continue my research in wound healing and infection. He transferred a $40,000 research grant that allowed me to support two laboratory technicians who came with me from Minnesota to Virginia. Moreover, he gave me half of his laboratory equipment, allowing me to set up my research laboratory. My multidisciplinary research studies have been instrumental in my development of a new emergency department, burn center and trauma center at the University of Virginia Health Sciences Center.

Create an academic culture that is friendly to learning.

Dr. Wangensteen had often told me that the chief responsibility of heads of department was to ". . . create an atmosphere friendly to learning." The role of the professor has been defined by others as that of teacher, clinician and investigator. He explained to me that, "his experience would suggest that two other items for heads of department should be added: 1) sideline cheerleader and 2) regimental water-carrier. My great friend, Dean Elias Potter, was wont to say that the best dean he knew was Gunga Din, Rudyard Kipling's regimental water-carrier. Above all these enumerated functions, however, it is my feeling that the most important concern of a department head is to create in his department and school an atmosphere friendly to learning. He must have the willingness to recognize every type of talent and ability and encourage people of promise. He must be the professor of the open door, easily accessible to his students, residents and his associates."

His Saturday morning conference was an important ritual for conducting the educational program in his department. Regularly in attendance were members of the departments of radiology and pathology. These conferences often served as exciting debates between various factions involved in the heated discussion. This crossfire often disturbed visitors accustomed to more genteel presentations. Dr. Wangensteen attended regularly and sat in the top row of the amphitheater near the door. He rarely participated in the debates unless he felt that a faculty member was taking unfair advantage of a resident, at which time he would intervene to stop the debate. He felt that, "The clinical conference, in which students, house officers and faculty participate, is probably the best teaching exercise in our medical schools today. We need to make the clinical pathological conference, as Churchill, of Boston, has so aptly remarked, less of a guessing game and more of a critical review directed at ascertaining whether the therapeutic course prescribed and followed was the best that could have been offered the patient. In other words, how much better, if at all, was post-mortem wisdom than anti-mortem vision. It must be heartening to undergraduate medical students to see how fallible their professors are. It must be even more reassuring to them to hear their teachers confess their errors, pointing out how, at various stages in the illness, a more astute and sensitive appraisal of the situation might have had a better and happier ending. Conferences, conducted with the greatest candor, in which the spirit of discussion is directed at the determination of how the milk was spilled, not who was responsible for spilling it, produced an atmosphere, I believe, in which

Dr. C. Walton Lillehei, a man undaunted by personal illness who became the father of modern open heart surgery.

students are most likely to be imbued with a passion for the pursuit of knowledge. In the lively leaven of an atmosphere fostering inquiry, no one was afraid to come forward with a novel idea, no matter how strange or unfamiliar it may have sounded. In the crucible of experiment and with friendly doubting Thomases looking on, the new idea could be given the acid test. The stages of a new idea are multiple. Many are still-born. But every new suggestion deserves at least a trial of being blown upon in the hope there may be sparks in the ashes."

We can especially appreciate Dr. Wangensteen's role as teacher and consummate physician by reflecting on his treatment of one of his patients, Clarence Walton Lillehei, who was the archetype of a brilliant teacher of surgery. He exemplified the kind of personality one needed, with resilience and self-confidence, a man undaunted by failure.[3] He began his surgical residency with Dr. Wangensteen in 1946. His residency consisted of 3-½ years of clinical training and a 1-year research fellowship with the noted cardiovascular physiologist, Dr. Maurice Visscher. Dr. Wangensteen considered Dr. Lillehei to be one of his finest residents destined to have a brilliant career in academic surgery. He anticipated that Dr. Lillehei would join his surgical faculty after completing his chief residency to continue his academic career.

During his chief residency, Dr. Lillehei faced a personal illness that could have dramatically changed his academic dreams. While making surgical patient care rounds with Dr. David State, a faculty member, his associate inadvertently noticed a swelling over Dr. Lillehei's left parotid gland, the large salivary gland within the left cheek. Believing that this swelling represented a possible tumor, Dr. State recommended the removal of the swelling to Dr. Lillehei. Dr. Lillehei agreed with the recommendation and asked Dr. State to perform the operative procedure. On February 9, 1950, Dr. State performed surgery on Dr. Lillehei and found ". . . a well-circumscribed tumor occupying the central portion of the superficial lobe of the parotid gland. There was a small lymph node in the deep portion of the gland." Frozen sections of the tumor revealed it to be a benign tumor or possibly a large lymph node. A superficial lobectomy of the salivary gland was undertaken with the specimen being sent to surgical pathology for careful microscopic examination. Dr. Lillehei made a rapid recovery from the surgery and returned to continue his chief residency training, with the expectation that the tumor was benign.

When the pathologist, Dr. Hebbel, found that the tumor was malignant (lymphosarcoma), State went to Dr. Wangensteen for his sage advice. It was Dr. Wangensteen's belief that Dr. Lillehei should undergo further surgery in three months to four months, at which time any further tumor would have reached the lymph nodes and could be removed. In addition, he said, "There was no virtue in telling Dr. Lillehei about all this at this time." He felt it best to acquaint Dr. Lillehei about the presence of the cancer only about the time the operation should be undertaken. Otherwise, he felt, "We might be stampeded into getting radiation therapy without further surgery." Dr. Wangensteen's rationale for his decision was based on his extensive experience in treating malignant tumors of the digestive tract that convinced him of the superiority of surgery over radiation therapy. He felt that, "Surgical excision, as drastic as it is, would be the better procedure."

In the hospital record, Dr. Wangensteen wrote the following note: "On Thursday, May 25, 1950, Dr. State and I informed Dr. Lillehei of the situation. It was then 3-½ months since the first procedure. He agreed to take the matter under advisement as to what should be done. Both Dr. State and I inclined to the thought that excision of the parotid gland, radical dissection of the neck and a dissection of the lymph nodes around the heart (mediastinum) would be the procedure of choice. Dr. Lillehei, after thinking the matter over, and I believe after consulting the literature, felt that surgery was probably the best procedure." In planning for surgery, Dr. Wangensteen assembled a team of surgeons whose surgical skills were recognized throughout the world. This multidisciplinary team would often be called together to care for high-profile individuals like royalty, heads of state, members of congress and celebrities who were given special attention because of their notoriety. In this case, these celebrated surgeons were brought together only by Dr. Wangensteen to care for this unknown surgical resident. Dr. David State was asked to join the team because he was a respected and skilled surgeon who had enormous experience in performing radical surgery on patients with cancer of the head and neck. Dr. F. John Lewis and Dr. Richard Varco were already recognized as surgical pioneers as they were two of the first individuals daring enough to operate within the chest cavity. Dr. Wangensteen was the ideal choice to head the team because he was a leader in cancer surgery. On June 1, 1950, Dr. State began the operation by removing the entire parotid gland, being careful to preserve the nerve that innervates muscles of facial expression. This extensive surgery left a sizable, notable depression in Dr. Lillehei's left cheek. Dr. State then proceeded to remove the large muscle extending from the jawbone down to the collarbone with the underlying lymph nodes draining the salivary glands. This radical dissection also left a noticeable deep defect in the left side of his neck. Under Dr. Wangensteen's guidance, Drs. Varco and Lewis traveled into the chest cavity to remove all of the lymph nodes surrounding his heart. In those days, this surgical adventure was similar to landing on the moon, occurring during the infancy of chest surgery and before the development of open heart surgery. As you can imagine, this dramatic surgical event left Dr. Lillehei with a noticeable cosmetic deformity. His head and neck were transformed from the appearance of a midwestern fearless hero to a young man with a sunken cheek and a narrow neck. This young surgeon could not hide his illness — now he had to wear it. At the peak of his surgical residency training program, Dr. Lillehei had a *life-defining experience*, a potentially fatal cancer. One month after surgery, Dr. Lillehei underwent 12 radiation treatments of his neck. His illness and subsequent radical treatments caused him to be *present in the moment* to his own mortality. Being faced with his own physical deformity, many physicians would retreat to less demanding professional occupations that would allow them to spend more time with their loved ones and smell the roses. With the help of his beloved mentor, Dr. Owen Wangensteen, he turned this personal crisis into an opportunity.

After radiation, Drs. Lillehei and Wangensteen never spoke about the young resident's future. Because Dr. Wangensteen had promised him a position on the faculty, he expected that Dr. Lillehei would accept this position. Dr. Wangensteen saw in his heart no disfigurement in Dr. Lillehei's appearance. Consequently, he pronounced through his own example that the department and the patients were to ignore Dr. Lillehei's physical deformity. His beloved vision of Dr. Lillehei was adopted by everyone. One year later, Dr. Wangensteen successfully championed Dr. Lillehei for promotion to an academic position of Associate Professor; this promotion is usually achieved by a faculty member within a three-year to seven-year time interval. Dr. Wangensteen confided in me that he believed that this early promotion of Dr. Lillehei would serve as a source of encouragement to him and reflect the University's commitment to his academic career.

Dr. Lillehei's major academic interest focused on children with congenital heart disorders, the "blue babies." At this time, the vast numbers of children with congenital heart disorders could not survive to adulthood. Most surgeons thought it impossible to do heart surgery successfully without the patient dying during the operative procedure. To address many of these diseases or malformations, the surgeon would have to cut into the heart and open it up in order to correct the specific problem. To achieve this *goal*, surgeons would have to overcome a seemingly insurmountable problem. The heart would have to be stopped from beating and drained from blood, during which time, the brain would be deprived of oxygen. Within two minutes to four minutes of oxygen deprivation, the brain would suffer irreversible damage.

Bill Bigelow, a young Canadian surgeon, reflected on this challenging problem in the early 1950s. He became intrigued with the phenomenon of hibernation, a state adopted by many animals in his frigid part of the world. During the lengthy winters, the hibernating animals survived for months without food by significantly reducing the metabolic needs of their hearts. Taking this insight from nature, Bigelow came up with the first workable proposal for performing open heart surgery. Bigelow found that when dogs' body temperatures were cooled, open heart surgery could be done for ten minutes without a pumping heart; four minutes is the maximum time that the brain can withstand oxygen deprivation at normal body temperature.

Dr. F. John Lewis, a powerful problem-solver, who had previously removed the lymph nodes from Dr. Lillehei's chest, enlisted the help of Dr. Lillehei in a pioneering and historic cardiothoracic procedure. They believed that Bigelow had a revolutionary approach to open heart surgery. For about a year, Dr. Lewis performed cardiac surgery on laboratory animals using hypothermia. Lewis, after doing a considerable number of successful cardiac surgical procedures in animals subjected to hypothermia, resolved to try it on humans and Dr. Lillehei assisted him. On September 2, 1952, Lewis and Lillehei performed the world's first successful operation within the open human heart under direct vision. Jacquie Johnson, a 5-year-old girl with a hole in her heart (atrial secundum defect), was wrapped in a cooling blanket until her body temperature decreased to 81° Fahrenheit. Clamping the inflow to her heart and emptying it of blood (inflow stasis), they opened up the slowly beating heart and quickly sewed up the hole inside her heart. This breathtaking operative procedure took five-and-a-half minutes, an unprecedented length of time for a patient to survive without blood circulating throughout the brain. With the repaired heart working properly for the first time in her life, she was immersed in a bath of warm water to bring her body temperature back to normal. Modern heart surgery had arrived! After surgery, Lillehei said to Lewis, "This is it, John. We're into the heart to stay." It was a *defining moment* in the history of surgery. A girl facing certain death would now live and grow up to have two normal children of her own.

Such operations soon became routine at the University of Minnesota Hospitals and news of the successes spread rapidly throughout the world. Hypothermia with inflow stasis proved to be excellent for babies born with holes in their hearts and for isolated congenital heart valve strictures. However, failure was uniform when hypothermia was applied to more complex lesions. Surgeons opened hearts and found these complex defects couldn't be repaired in ten minutes, the outer limit of successful cardiac surgery using hypothermia. With the clock ticking away, they found themselves unable to finish what they had started.

The experience with hypothermia reconfirmed the need for an artificial heart-lung machine, known as a pump oxygenator, that allowed intracardiac surgery to be performed safely for a sufficient time to correct the complex defects. The first successful use of a pump oxygenator for intracardiac operations occurred on May 6, 1953, when Dr. John Gibbon successfully closed a hole in the heart of an 18-year-old girl. Gibbon was never able to repeat this one success with an atrial septal defect or with more complex congenital heart defects. After two more unsuccessful operations, Dr. Gibbon became discouraged and did not use his pump oxygenator again. Between 1951 and 1954, more than 20 reported (and many more unreported) attempts were made worldwide to utilize pump oxygenators in humans for correction of more complex malformations. None were successful, and 100% of the patients died in the operating room. In all of their reported attempts at clinical heart operation, there was a common scenario: nearly universal failure when the pump oxygenator was applied to humans. Consequently, many of the experienced investigators concluded with seemingly impeccable logic that the problems were not with the pump oxygenators. Rather, they came to believe that the sick human heart, ravaged by failure, could not possibly be expected to tolerate the magnitude of the operation required and then recover with good results. Thus, discouragement and pessimism about the future of open-heart surgery were widespread.

In his experimental work of controlled cross-circulation in dogs, Dr. Lillehei connected the venous and arterial circulation in such a manner that one dog's circulation served temporarily as an oxygenator and a single, mechanical substitute for the heart of another dog without the need for a complex, conventional pump oxygenator unavailable at that time. As the experiments progressed, it soon became apparent that the dogs undergoing a 30-minute interval of controlled cross-circulation not only survived at a far greater percentage, but also recovered more rapidly compared with the earlier dogs he had observed using the pump oxygenator for the same period of time. The differences were truly astonishing, and for the first time, he realized that cross-circulation might be the simple and effective clinical method for intracardiac operations for which he was searching. He viewed controlled cross-circulation as a near perfect oxygenator system because it simulated a "temporary placenta," which serves as the heart and lung for the unborn baby. This salient fact was undoubtedly extremely important to the significant accomplishments that were to be achieved later in humans. He suspected that there were massive chemical disturbances evoked by the pump oxygenator about which little was known and that by temporarily instituting a "placental circulation," he might minimize or even correct these disturbances to permit successful, otherwise impossible, operations.

In a valiant attempt that no hospital ethics committee would allow to take place today, Lillehei began trying to extend the length of a young child's open heart operation past ten minutes by attaching the child's blood vessels to his parent's. On March 26, 1954, Dr. Lillehei performed intracardiac surgery with controlled cross-circulation using the father with the same blood type as his 1-year-old son with a large hole in his heart (ventricular septal defect). The father was the human heart- lung machine for his baby boy. If anything went wrong, the father, as well as his son's, life would be at stake. The thought of taking a healthy individual to the operating room to serve as a human pump oxygenator, however small the risks were, was considered by some critics at that time as unacceptable, even "immoral" as one prominent surgeon was heard to say. Some others, skilled in the art of criticism, were quick to point out that the proposed operation was the first in all surgical history to have the potential for a 200% mortality rate! This first cross-circulation intracardiac surgery was fortunately successful. In one circumstance the patient as well as the child died. As the heroic surgeons watched in horror, an air bubble sped through the connecting clear plastic tubing into the parent's veins causing a fatal heart attack. He repeated this procedure another 46 times; the survival rate of the desperately ill children was 63% with no further deaths of the parents serving as the human pump. All of Lillehei's surgical procedures corrected complex heart anomalies that were previously inoperable.

Thanks to Dr. Lillehei's daring surgery, this baby boy as well as many other children are alive today. They are living proof that very sick hearts could survive open heart surgery. Yet these few cases had become a forgotten episode in surgery's history because few surgeons had the technical ability to use Dr. Lillehei's method. Within 12 months, Lillehei was able to replace the human beating heart-lung "machine" with a simple disposable oxygenator that had an enormous impact upon the growth of open heart surgery. The originator of this pivotal piece of medical machinery was Dr. Dick De Wall, a surgical resident whom Dr. Wangensteen had successfully rescued from the certain doom of a poor academic record in medical school.

Dr. Wangensteen believed that the selection of candidates for surgical residency should be based on their interest in surgery as well as their academic record. He met with all candidates for admission to the surgical training program who had already been recommended by a committee appointed to examine the candidates' qualifications. The Dean of the Graduate School of the University of Minnesota denied admission of candidates for surgical residency who had displayed a poor academic record in medical school. This was his reason for denying an appointment to Dr. De Wall to the surgical residency program. So impressed was Dr. Wangensteen with Dr. De Wall's promise in surgical research, and determined to provide the young man with the opportunity to show that potential, Dr. Wangensteen appointed Dr. DeWall as a diener in the dog laboratory. He explained to Dr. DeWall that the responsibility of a diener was to clean the dog cages and remove any excrement. However, he assured Dr. DeWall that this position was in title alone because he would not have any of those housecleaning responsibilities. He pointed out that an additional incentive in taking this position was a salary that was identical to the surgical residents. Most importantly, his acceptance of this position would allow him to pursue his *goal* of participating in the surgical research program. Dr. DeWall worked tirelessly and, within one year, had built a safe heart-lung machine that used as an unorthodox but very simple way of getting oxygen into the blood – by bubbling it in.

Bubbling oxygen in the blood to oxygenate it was the one method that all authorities at the time said could not possibly work, predicting that it would cause death uniformly by air embolism. Dr. Lillehei asked Dr. DeWall to devise an effective, foolproof method to get the bubbles out rapidly. With a few tubes, clips and some antifoam silicone from a mayonnaise manufacturer to get the bubbles out, Dr. DeWall built a simple disposable oxygenator. It would become the most popular oxygenator in the world. In this exciting climate, the University of Minnesota became a mecca for aspiring heart surgeons. Although Dr. Lillehei is frequently acknowledged as the "Father of open-heart surgery" and as the surgeon who first corrected most every cardiac defect, he still indicates that his greatest pride comes from the training of over 150 cardiac surgeons from 40 different countries from around the world. His training program had resulted in a *societal transformation* in which patients with injured or diseased hearts could benefit from his revolutionary open heart surgery. Many of his trainees have become world leaders in the field of cardiac surgery, and two have become household names: Christiaan Bernard, later to become the first man to transplant the human heart, and Norman Shumway, now the premier heart transplant surgeon. Dr. Lillehei's pioneering contributions to cardiac surgery were the catalyst for amazing advances in surgery. In under a decade, the heart had been conquered. In

1998, 200,000 open heart operations were done worldwide; that is about 500 every 24 hours.

It is important to remember that Dr. Lillehei's monumental accomplishments in medicine occurred in Dr. Wangensteen's academic village in which innovation through research springs eternal. Dr. Wangensteen guided Dr. Lillehei through the challenges of his illness, accepting the necessity for a paternalistic role. I realize that the physician is faced with a challenging balancing act when trying to make decisions that are medically sound as well as loyal to the patient's wishes. Dr. Wangensteen made his medical decisions on the basis of his vast breadth of scientific information, keeping hope eternal for finding resolution to the problem. He also provided the emotional support that allowed Dr. Lillehei to revolutionize surgical care. Today, 48 years later, Dr. Lillehei jokingly comments that, "Dr. Wangensteen's radical surgery on me frightened the cancer away."

This inspirational relationship between the physician-as-patient (Lillehei) and his doctor (Wangensteen), is the antithesis of the destructive components of many other physician-as-patient experiences. Many physician-as-patients recall the alienation of being a patient. Dr. Sanes[4] had seen cancer from the viewpoint of a medical student and a Buffalo, New York pathologist. Later as a patient, he realized how much he still had to learn as a physician. He remembered his months of being a patient: "But if I rejoiced in the blessing of the sun, I found I was avoided by the non-patients in the gardens – by the students, nurses, visitors who came there. I was set apart, we were set apart, we patients in white nightgowns and avoided clearly, though unconsciously, like lepers. . .. I realized how I myself, in health, in the past had shuddered away from patients quite unconsciously, never realizing it for a moment." Isolation is even stronger when the patient has cancer. Dr. Sanes found that, along with physical death, the patient with cancer ". . . faces social death, as an active, contributing, accepted member of society. The latter may seem a much worse fate to him." Others have the feeling that their colleagues continue to regard them as different even after they have recovered because they have been tainted with the scent of death, the scent of weakness.

How often the case has been, however, that success has not been in spite of a handicap, but because of a handicap. The account of William Ernest Henley's (1849–1907) battle with his illness has provided hope and inspiration for the world.[5] As a boy living in Edinburgh, he had tubercular arthritis that necessitated the amputation of his left leg at age 18. He was advised at age 24 that amputation of his remaining leg was inevitable. While accepting the grim verdict of the loss of one leg, he could not imagine making his way with none. His right leg was saved only by the skill and radical new method of the surgeon Joseph Lister, whom he sought out in Edinburgh. Forced to stay in an infirmary there for 18 months (1873–1875), he began writing poetry about hospital life that established his poetic reputation. Dating from the same period is his most famous poem, "Invictus":

> Out of the night that covers me,
> Black as the Pit from pole to pole,
> I thank whatever gods may be
> For my unconquerable soul.
> In the fell clutch of circumstance
>
> I have not winced nor cried aloud.
> Under the bludgeonings of chance
> Me head is bloody, but unbowed.
>
> Beyond this place of wrath and tears
> Looms but the Horror of the shade,
> And yet the menace of the years
> Finds, and shall find, me unafraid.
>
> It matters not how strait the gate
> How charged with punishments the scroll,
> I am master of my fate:
> I am the captain of my soul

"Invictus," unconquerable, invincible, indestructible, is the only reply I know to give those who would advise to shun the call to solve the impossible problem.

An inspirational plastic surgeon, Dr. Erle Peacock, has developed the same focused and tireless attitude in solving patients' illnesses. He explained this to me using a familiar parable. He developed the philosophy and shrugging motions of the old horse that accidentally fell into the well. The well was not too deep, and it had been dry for many years. The horse was not too good, and so the farmer decided the best way to settle the situation was to throw dirt into the well until he covered the horse and the well at the same time. With each shovel-full of dirt that was shrugged off and stamped under foot, the horse raised himself higher in the well. Before long the horse was standing on dry land because he refused to be buried. Dr. Peacock's inherent message was learn the shrugging, stamping motion, and refuse to be buried.

As we reflect on the heroic accomplishments of Drs. Lillehei and DeWall, there is a natural tendency to focus primarily on their revolutionary surgical advances rather than their own personal challenges. There is an inclination to associate heroic accomplishments with a heroic archetype that exhibits physical beauty and scholastic success. We often assume that these accomplishments are best achieved by individuals possessing personal physical characteristics that exemplify "specialness." Individuals with physical beauty, bodily strength, brilliant intellectual capabilities and extroverted personalities are destined to change the world, after all. Those unfortunate souls harnessed with a serious illness that has the scent of death are often advised to hide their sorrow in a closet, fearing that it will cause discomfort to the public as well as themselves. While hiding information about personal illness brings comfort to society, this conspiracy of silence will usually supply such power to the illness that it immobilizes the patient. Unfortunately, an illness that results or causes a physical deformity becomes a warning signal to a society that often socially isolates the patient. Because the illness can no longer be hidden in the closet, the patient must deal continually with the penetrating eyes of society who desperately want to know, but are afraid to ask. This conspiracy of silence is uncomfortably interrupted by the voices of two-year-olds asking, "What happened to you?!" This inquisition is viewed by most as being impolite and therefore the innocent questioner is silenced with apologies from embarrassed parents.

In our elite educational institutions, the merit of a human being is often judged by scholastic grades. Some educational institutions receive so many applicants that they don't have sufficient staff to interview each of them. By abandoning the interview process, decisions are made on the basis of scholastic achievement complemented by the applicants' written answers to open-ended questions. This process of student selection is blind to the student with a disability, but expeditiously eliminates students whose records are branded with a C, D, or F. Today, the F grade becomes intimately associated with the person's character and potential and denotes inappropriately that the person is a failure rather than an indication that they did not successfully complete the course. Realizing society's views toward disability as well as the educational system's obsession with grades, I would seriously question if C. Walton Lillehei and Dick DeWall would have changed the world in other academic settings other than in Wangensteen's academic village. Realizing the enormous impact of Dr. Wangensteen's unique educational system on surgery, it is important to identify the educational principles of his program that fostered empowerment of the human soul. If these principles were replicated throughout the world, I believe that the cultural values of society would be transformed into one that celebrates each person as the prince and princess of possibilities.

Dr. Wangensteen was very concerned that our childlike dreams would be buried by individuals who remain convinced that the impossible remains impossible. James Russell Lowell (1818–1891), an American poet, centered his work on making the individual sole sponsor of himself and on self-mastery in the midst of greed and personal temptation.[6] In his poem, "Aladdin," he warns us that the child's creative dreams and imagination can be smothered by the adult's search for power and financial reward:

> When I was a beggarly boy,
> And lived in a cellar damp,
> I had not a friend nor a toy,
> But I had Aladdin's lamp;
> When I could not sleep for the cold,
> I had fire enough in my brain,
> And builded, with roofs of gold,
> My beautiful castles in Spain!
>
> Since then I have toiled day and night,
> Have money and power good store,
> But I'd give all my lamps of silver bright
> For the one that is mine no more;
> Take, Fortune, whatever you may choose,
> You gave, and may snatch again;
> I have nothing, 'twould pain me to lose,
> For I own no more castles in Spain!

Dr. Owen H. Wangensteen became the greatest teacher in surgery during the 20th century because he had a clear vision of his *goal* as a teacher: to train teachers of surgery, rather than practicing surgeons. He realized that the success of his program was dependent on his establishment of a unique culture in which each of his students perceived that they were the princes and princesses of possibilities.[7] He designed an academic curriculum that allowed his students to succeed as teachers. This curriculum included research experiences that would allow each student to receive a doctoral degree (Ph.D.) in the graduate program of the University as well as clinical surgical training sufficient to receive his board certification in surgery. In addition, Dr. Wangensteen realized that he needed a critical mass (eight residents/year) to undertake multidisciplinary investigations that would solve important clinical problems. In the absence of state funding for his training program, he became a successful fund-raiser gaining sufficient funds to pay resident salaries and sponsor research. Residents completing the training program had sufficient academic credentials that allowed them to receive tenured faculty positions in surgical educational programs in other universities. Realizing that the graduates' journey to success in teaching can be a tortuous one, he remained available to them for guidance and advice. I believe that these lessons learned from this gifted teacher will be easily appreciated by any student or teacher involved in higher education and also will be a source of inspiration to anyone involved in teaching outside the confines of an academic institution.

3

Student's Journey

"The teacher who succeeds in instilling a love and lust for learning in his students projects his influence to unborn generations."

Dr. Owen H. Wangensteen

By themselves, the pieces of my life do not seem to fit together, but my experiences have taught me that there are no accidents. The events in my life had to happen. Throughout my life, I have been given clues that pointed me in a direction that I was supposed to head. It will come as no surprise to you that my mother's illness of recurrent intestinal obstruction had a profound influence on my life and served as my guide on my *student's* journey to Dr. Wangensteen.[1] Her illness was my *life-defining experience* that caused me to be *present in the moment* to her severe abdominal cramping pain and her fears of another attack of intestinal obstruction. Her pain became so great for me that it consumed my childhood and adolescent experiences .

The pain of her illness caused me to identify one of my most important *goals* in life: *to prevent intestinal obstruction.* When I was given the choice of watching her clutch her abdomen during the attacks of dreadful colicky pain versus escaping to college at age 15 to begin my accelerated education, I reluctantly chose the early admission college program option without concerns about my immaturity in the adult collegiate environment. Disinterested in the socialization activities of college, I successfully pursued an early admission program to New York University College of Medicine. By age 22, I was a full-fledged doctor who was trying subconsciously to find the path to curing my mother's illness, recurrent intestinal obstruction caused by the stringlike adhesive bands that blocked her intestines.

I fortuitously found the secrets of my mother's illness in Dr. Owen Wangensteen's training program in the University of Minnesota. He helped me transform her catastrophic illness into a *life-transforming opportunity*. Because Dr. Wangensteen was the world-renowned expert for treating patients with intestinal obstruction, literally hundreds of patients with this disease flocked to Minnesota for his wise advice and counsel. Dr. Wangensteen taught me how to diagnose and treat patients like my mother, with intestinal obstruction and identified a pathway for my successful career in academic surgery. My special commitment to these patients with intestinal obstruction served to compensate for my childhood sadness about my mother's devastating attacks of recurrent intestinal obstruction. As a child, I could do nothing but console my mother. With Dr. Wangensteen's training, I now had the powers to bring miraculous cures to patients with these devastating illnesses.

Moreover, Dr. Wangensteen selected a topic for my future research investigations that would direct me to plastic surgery.[1] He believed that my research in plastic surgery would identify the causes of these stringlike bands that compressed my mother's intestines. Because Dr. Wangensteen and other scientists had incriminated the powder on surgical gloves as a major cause of adhesion formation, he encouraged me to revolutionize surgery and develop powder-free gloves. I eventually called these glove powders "deadly dust" to acknowledge their enormous impact on my mother's life. He also enlightened me, an aspiring plastic surgeon, on important personal survival techniques in academic surgery. After reading this chapter, I believe you will understand the profound impact that Dr. Wangensteen had on my life.

At the University of Virginia School of Medicine, I modeled my approach to education after that taught to me by Dr. Wangensteen. My research continued to be a multidisciplinary effort, involving distinguished scientists who formed the foundation for a strong and productive research laboratory. These innovative scientists were *powerful problem-solvers*. It is a pleasure and honor to acknowledge Dr. George T. Rodeheaver, research professor of plastic surgery, and Dr. John G. Thacker, professor of mechanical and aerospace engineering, who have been my partners in research programs for the last 25 years.

Dr. Rodeheaver is an organic chemist who has made numerous scientific contributions that have received national recognition. Recently, the Board of Visitors of the University has established an endowed chair for a basic scientist in the Department of Plastic Surgery. The endowment for this chair was established by generous gifts from my colleagues and friends who honored me by having the chair named the Richard F. Edlich

Research Professor of Plastic Surgery. This endowed chair is the first and only chair for a basic scientist in a Division or Department of Plastic Surgery in the world. I was delighted that Dr. Rodeheaver was selected by the Board of Visitors of the University of Virginia as the first Richard F. Edlich Research Professor of Plastic Surgery. Dr. Thacker has had an illustrious career in mechanical engineering and is now Vice-Chairman of the Department of Mechanical and Aerospace Engineering.

The mission of our research laboratory has been to develop *scientific products and drugs that allow wounds to heal without infection, or adhesion and scar formation.* Our research has involved literally hundreds of undergraduate students, medical students, postdoctoral fellows and residents who enthusiastically brought their energy and scholarship into our investigations. In our academic journey, we realized that the contribution of our intellectual progeny will far exceed our own, a reward that is the essence of teaching.

The results of our research have far exceeded our expectations. We have identified numerous innovative surgical techniques that prevent infection as well as adhesion formation. These adhesions are the same stringlike strands that compressed my mother's intestines, causing intestinal obstruction. These surgical techniques have been incorporated into teaching curricula entitled, "Scientific Basis of Wound Closure Techniques," "Scientific Basis of Vascular (blood vessel) Anastomosis," and "Scientific Basis of Intestinal Anastomosis," that include a manual and a videotape training program being used to teach surgeons and physicians throughout the world. These educational curricula have been approved for continuing medical education credits by the Dannemiller Memorial Foundation and are sponsored by my close friend, Leon Hirsch, President of the United States Surgical Corporation. With the advent of these programs, I believe that surgery is on the threshold of a new horizon in which wounds of the skin, intestine and vessels can be repaired without infection and adhesions.

Our multidisciplinary research program has focused on four important clinical problems: medicine's deadly dust, dirty lacerations and cuts, minor and severe burns and chronic wounds and pressure ulcers.

Medicine's Deadly Dust

When surgical gloves were introduced at the turn of the century, they were sterilized by boiling and could only be donned by pulling the rubber gloves over wet hands.[1] Because the wet hands of the surgical staff became macerated under the occlusive cover of the rubber glove, predisposing to severe skin inflammation (dermatitis), surgeons searched for a dry lubricant that would facilitate donning and prevent the gloves from sticking together during the pressurized steam sterilization process (autoclaving). An early lubricant, a powder made of *Lycopodium* spores (club moss), was identified as causing foreign body responses, including adhesions and granulomas. Talcum powder (hydrous magnesium silicate), a nonabsorbable lubricant, was also implicated in the production of a tumorlike mass, granuloma, and stringlike fibers, adhesions, in the abdominal cavity. In a study in 1947, Dr. Edwin Lehman, Professor and Chairman of the Department of Surgery and Obstetrics at the University of Virginia, identified what appeared to be an acceptable alternative to talc - cornstarch powder.[2] He also verified the increasing evidence that talcum powder was a dangerous disease-promoting factor in human surgery. He found that cornstarch powder was completely absorbed from the abdominal cavity without any demonstrated inflammation, and it produced no adhesions whatsoever. Because it was a cornstarch powder, it was taken up by the abdominal cavity and metabolized like any ingested starch. Currently, cornstarch is the lubricant found on most surgical and examination gloves used by healthcare workers. However, experimental and clinical studies, performed in our laboratory as well as many others, in the last 50 years have continually documented dangerous side effects of this absorbable lubricant. Likely in response to concerns about adverse effects caused by cornstarch, the Food and Drug Administration (FDA) in 1971 required manufacturers to place warning labels on glove packages that stated that glove-users should remove cornstarch from the glove surfaces by wiping the gloves with a wet sponge, towel, or by using another effective method.

Most surgeons still have an unfounded confidence in cornstarch and mistakenly believe that it is safe. While it was an unquestionable advance in the 1950s, subsequent scientific studies have demonstrated that cornstarch promotes illnesses by two different mechanisms. First, our laboratory has demonstrated that cornstarch acts as a foreign body in the wound that elicits an exaggerated inflammatory response and interferes with the tissue's defenses against infection. When cornstarch contaminates human tissue, it promotes the development of wound infection. The presence of small amounts of cornstarch causes swelling of the wound and enhances bacterial growth that results in infection. When cornstarch gains access to the abdominal cavity, it can cause a tumorlike mass, granuloma, stringlike fibers (adhesions) and inflammation of the lining of the abdominal cavity (peritonitis). The development of cornstarch-induced adhesions can result in intestinal obstruction, infertility and pelvic pain. Despite these recognized dangers of cornstarch, most surgeons ignore the FDA warning on glove packages and fail to remove cornstarch from their gloves before surgery.

The second mechanism by which cornstarch on gloves causes illness is based on its role as a carrier for latex allergens. Reported reactions to latex included inflammation of the hands beneath the gloves, hives, runny nose, asthma and anaphylactic shock. These life- threatening reactions are very similar to those encountered in sensitized patients who are stung by bees. The development of the reaction to latex has been linked to the individual's production of antibodies to natural latex when exposed to this substance. The frequency of latex allergy increased dramatically with the introduction of Universal Precautions, outlined by the Centers for Disease Control and Prevention (CDC) to minimize the risk of an occupational exposure to the human immunodeficiency virus (HIV) that causes acquired immune deficiency syndrome (AIDS). The CDC required that health professionals wear gloves to protect themselves from contact with blood and secretions of their patients. Since 1987, the frequency of glove usage increased dramatically, currently approaching 10 billion gloves per year. The demand for latex gloves exceeded the production capability of manufacturers with high quality control standards. Consequently, hospitals purchased a large number of latex gloves from manufacturers with inadequate quality control standards to meet demand. Their manufacturing processes used in these gloves did not successfully remove the soluble latex proteins. It was believed that these cheaper gloves with higher concentrations of soluble latex proteins caused allergic reactions in many healthcare workers and patients during the 1980s. Despite this revelation of the high concentration of water-soluble latex proteins, these highly allergenic gloves are still being used today as routine surgical and examination gloves.

In 1992, Drs. Donald H. Beezhold and William C. Beck of the Guthrie Foundation in Sayre, Pennsylvania, demonstrated that the cornstarch on surgical gloves when combined with the soluble latex proteins, became a potentially reactive allergy-causing particle.[3] Complex antigens, such as those composed of both protein and starch components, have been shown to stimulate the immune system to a greater degree than highly purified antigens. They warned that this significant interaction between latex protein and cornstarch powders not only exacerbated allergy, but also promoted the development of latex-sensitization. When healthcare providers put on and remove surgical and medical examination gloves, the starch powder particles with their attached protein easily become airborne and can be inhaled over a period of many hours. Latex-sensitive patients who inhale these latex protein-cornstarch particles suffer severe allergic reactions.

When cornstarch was demonstrated to be a vector for the latex allergy epidemic, this finding became the strongest argument for the use of powder-free gloves. This observation, combined with the extensive experimental and clinical studies demonstrating that cornstarch was toxic to all tissues of our body, should provide convincing evidence for the FDA to ban cornstarch powder from surgical gloves. To this end, our laboratory has devised a five-pronged approach to convince the FDA to ban this dangerous powder. This decision would be a dynamic *societal transformation program* that would protect other individuals, like my mother, from the dangerous effects of medicine's deadly dust. Our strategy included (1) biomechanical performance studies on surgical and examination gloves, (2) publication of *Medicine's Deadly Dust*, (3) petition to the FDA, (4) a consumer website identifying the powder-free hospitals in the United States, and (5) a television documentary.

Working with Dr. John Thacker, a team of talented students devised a battery of reproducible tests that evaluated the handling characteristics of surgical and examination gloves. Their comprehensive studies demonstrated that healthcare workers can easily put on (don) powder-free surgical and examination gloves. In fact, the donning forces encountered by healthcare workers using powder-free gloves were comparable to those noted with powdered gloves, even with wet hands! Moreover, the tactile sensitivity of healthcare workers' hands covered by powder-free gloves were similar to that encountered in healthcare workers wearing powdered gloves. Finally, the resistance to needle penetration of powdered and powder-free surgical and examination gloves were not significantly different. These comprehensive experimental studies provided convincing evidence that powder-free gloves are a safe and effective substitute for the powder gloves.

Because the FDA has been reluctant to ban cornstarch from surgical and examination gloves, I enlisted the help of my talented colleagues, Dr. Julia Woods and Dr. Mary Jude Cox, to write a book, *Medicine's Deadly*

Dust, that highlights the dangers of these dusting powders and serves as a wake-up call to society.[1] With the advent of powder-free surgical and examination gloves, the use of powdered gloves is now an unacceptable and dangerous medical practice. Our book has had a positive impact on the University of Virginia Medical Center and Martha Jefferson Hospital in Charlottesville, Virginia, as well as 15 other hospitals in Virginia, causing them to decide to become powder-free hospitals. Today, hospitals throughout the country have developed this same responsible leadership and announced that they too will only use powder-free products. Kaiser Permanente, one of the most respected health maintenance operations in our country, announced that all of its hospitals will be powder-free by 1999! Despite this rapid transition to a powder-free healthcare environment, we realized that many hospitals continue to use powdered gloves that endanger their patients.

Because our book was not a catalyst for an FDA decision to ban glove powders, we have joined forces with Dr. Sidney Wolfe of the consumer watchdog, Public Citizen, to prepare and file a petition to the FDA demanding a ban on cornstarch on gloves. This petition was submitted to Dr. Michael Friedman, Lead Deputy Commissioner of the Food and Drug Administration, on January 7, 1998.

To further awaken society to this life-threatening healthcare problem, we developed a website providing a list of the powder-free hospitals using only powder-free products. This website, *www.deadlydust.com*, provides concise, accessible information outlining the dangers posed by the presence of cornstarch on medical gloves. More importantly, it directs website visitors with an interactive map which points them to the nearest powder-free hospital facility. By providing healthcare consumers with this information, they become partners with their doctors in their healthcare.

I am saddened that these scholarly efforts have still not convinced the FDA to ban powder from surgical and examination gloves. I attribute my failure to convince the FDA to take action to protect the healthcare worker against latex allergy to not having drawn an accurate picture of the pain of social and emotional isolation of individuals sensitized to latex. In other words, the decision-makers of the FDA have not been present to the *life-defining experiences* of individuals with latex allergy. Because a picture is worth a thousand words, I enlisted the help of the talented investigative reporter, Maria Hess, to prepare a television documentary on this healthcare crisis.

On February 26, 1998, PBS television aired the Hess documentary on the latex allergy epidemic in our country. It featured the talented dentists, Dr. Lise Borel and Dr. William Macchia, who eloquently described their latex allergies that ended their professional careers. This documentary also described the valiant efforts of Martha Jefferson Hospital in Virginia to become the second powder-free private hospital in our country. Their powder-free glove selection program was described in detail so that it could be replicated in other hospitals. Martha Jefferson Hospital's experience has been a catalyst for other hospitals in Virginia to follow its leadership role in healthcare. By the end of 1999, I predict that there will be more powder-free hospitals in Virginia than any other state in our country. As a result of the book, petition, website and television program, our vision of a powder-free healthcare environment in Virginia is rapidly coming to fruition.

However, our successes in Virginia are little consolation for other states. In a continuing effort to ban medicine's deadly dust in hospitals, I have enlisted the help of two dynamic healthcare leaders to transform our nation's healthcare system. Dr. Lise Borel has been a guiding force to stop this latex allergy epidemic. After developing a latex allergy, she turned this potentially life-threatening *catastrophic allergy into an opportunity* to end this epidemic. She formed a nonprofit organization called ELASTIC, Inc., that has members in 45 of the 50 states. Its mission is to educate the public on the latex allergy epidemic and provide information for hospitals regarding treatment of latex allergic patients. Another *goal* of the organization is to reduce the frequency of latex allergies by asking hospitals to use only powder-free gloves, as well as more latex-free gloves. Lise Borel has joined forces with Debra Atkins, another healthcare professional with latex allergy, to educate hospitals and the public about latex allergies. Debra is the editor of *Latex Allergy News*, which should be required reading for all health professionals, as well as patients with latex allergies. Lise Borel and Debra Atkins have allowed our society to be *present in the moment* to the catastrophic consequences of the latex allergy epidemic. They have invited society into their lives to witness the devastating effects of this epidemic. They both deserve the major credit for reducing the use of medicine's deadly dust. As a joint effort, members of ELASTIC, Inc., and I wrote a chain letter involving more than 500 individuals to Secretary of Health and Human Services, Donna Shalala, demanding that the FDA ban powder from examination and surgical gloves. Six months later, the Secretary has still not responded to any letter. The most likely reason for her failure to respond is that it takes more than 500 letters to catch her attention.

Dirty Lacerations and Cuts

Our scientific investigations were designed to bring advances to the patient's bedside and ultimately result in a clinical care center especially designed to treat these challenging problems. Our studies of the care of dirty cuts and lacerations ultimately provided the research and clinical expertise that allowed for the development of a trauma center at the University of Virginia Hospital. Some of the highlights of our studies of dirty wounds were the development of wound closure tapes, wound cleansing solutions and high-pressure irrigation.[4]

Until the advent of our collaborative research program between Minnesota Mining and Manufacturing (3-M), St. Paul, Minnesota, and our laboratory, most physicians either closed dirty wounds with sutures or left them open, allowing them to heal slowly without surgical closure. Because sutures are foreign bodies that damage the body's defenses, we conceived a closure technique that did not involve placement of a foreign body, like sutures, in the wound. Adhesive tape would be an ideal solution, but it had many drawbacks. Its cloth backing did not permit air passage, causing maceration and wetness of the underlying skin. Its rubber-based adhesive aggressively bonded to the skin, making it difficult to remove and uncomfortable for the patient. After discussing the need for a new wound closure tape with the healthcare division of 3-M, they devised a new tape backing that had pores, allowing transmission of air. Coverage of the skin with this microporous tape allowed transmission of air and drying of the underlying skin. A new adhesive was developed that maintained the tape's porosity and provided sufficient adhesion to the underlying skin, ensuring secure wound closure. This tape is called Reinforced Steri-Strip™ and remains the most popular wound closure tape in the world. To date, this tape has been used successfully in wound care in an estimated 1 billion patients. Subsequently, 3-M's healthcare division has grown from a team of four employees to 3,000 employees.

During the last century, physicians have been adding antiseptic agents, like iodine, pHisoHex, and mercurochrome, to dirty wounds to kill any surface bacteria. Our studies demonstrated that these antiseptic agents injured the tissue and the body defenses, thereby enhancing the incidence of infection. Consequently, we had to search for a wound cleansing soap that was so safe that it could be poured directly into a physician's eye. After a decade of study, we identified a soap (surfactant) that was so safe that it could be poured into your eye or given intravenously.[5] After it was approved by the FDA, it was marketed by Calgon-Vestal, St. Louis, Missouri, under the name of Shur-Clens™. It is important to acknowledge Dr. Leonard Kurtz, President of Deknatel, Inc. (Queens Village, New York), who shepherded this drug into the marketplace. Dr. Kurtz was a recognized expert in surgical devices who served as a gifted teacher and friend for more than 20 years. During the last decade, Shur-Clens™ has been used to wash dirty wounds in an estimated 20 million patients without a reported adverse side effect. It is now the accepted gold standard as a soap for wound cleansing in emergency departments and operating rooms. Despite the introduction of this safe product, some physicians continue to use toxic antiseptic agents to cleanse wounds. For such arrogant physicians who do not read current scientific literature, I would recommend that they pour the antiseptic agent into their eyes before it contacts the patient's wound.

Wound cleansing with a sterile saltwater solution was a time-honored concept in wound cleansing. Most surgeons believed that pouring sterile saltwater in sufficiently large quantities into the wound would rid it of bacteria. Pleased with this treatment, some surgeons commented that, "Dilution would be the end of pollution." Our studies demonstrated that pouring large amounts of saltwater into the wound did not successfully remove all bacteria and prevent infection.[6,7] Dr. John Thacker confirmed that irrigation with sterile saltwater delivered under high pressures (7 lbs/in^2) now could effectively remove bacteria and prevent wound infection. We realized that a physician's effort to remove bacteria from the wound was comparable to hitting a Ping-Pong® ball with a baseball bat out of a stadium, that is, you needed a lot of force. Today, high-pressure wound irrigation is used throughout the world to remove bacteria from wounds.

Minor and Severe Burns

Our research on the care of the burn wound was recognized by scientists throughout the world and convinced our medical center to develop a regional burn center directed by the Department of Plastic Surgery. Two notable studies undertaken by our research team dramatically improved the care of the burn patient. One investigation resulted in the development of an improved burn cream that prevents burn wound infection.

The other study examined the cause of burn injuries in Virginia, convincing us that the best treatment of burns was prevention!

Burn creams containing antibiotics are commonly used to prevent life-threatening infection of the burn wound. These creams contain either water-soluble carriers or carriers that are relatively insoluble in water. We favored the use of water-soluble carriers because they are easily applied and removed from the burn wound by washing with water. The insoluble carriers adhere rather aggressively to the burned skin and must be removed manually with a wetted gauze sponge, which causes considerable discomfort to the patient. During our use of the water-soluble burn creams in patients whose burns involved more than half of their body surface area, I was shocked to find that some patients were developing early loss of kidney function.[8] Four consecutive patients died this way. We enlisted the help of our skilled pathologists, Drs. David Bruns and Ben Sturgill, to find the cause. In their careful review of laboratory results, they identified the cause of kidney failure. The water-soluble burn creams contained a chemical, polyethylene glycol, that was being absorbed through the skin, causing kidney failure.

When we immediately converted to the use of the water-insoluble burn creams, we no longer encountered this chemical poisoning of the kidney. As you may suspect, the results of our scientific investigations documenting the danger of these water-soluble burn creams were highlighted in every newspaper and television program, causing the FDA to ban the use of water-soluble burn creams containing this chemical on patients whose burns covered large body surface areas. While our studies successfully eliminated the use of water-soluble burn creams, we now had to resort to the water-insoluble creams that caused severe pain to the patients during application and removal. Dr. Rodeheaver began his search for a safe, water-soluble alternative. In his early studies, he had noted that our safe wound cleanser, Shur-Clens™, became a gel in more concentrated solutions.[9,10] Because Shur-Clens™ had been used extensively and safely in millions of patients, he surmised that this gel could be used as a carrier for the burn cream. Studies in animals confirmed the safety and efficacy of this concentrated form of Shur-Clens™. Our preliminary clinical studies with this new, safe, water-soluble burn cream have been completed. Our clinical results with this new formulation were so impressive that this new water-soluble burn cream has replaced the water-insoluble burn creams in our medical center.

Our team of scientists completed a landmark study of the cause of burn injuries in Virginia that was supported by a grant from the Department of Health and Human Services.[11] I was shocked by the results of our findings, which documented that the most important predictor of the cause of burn injury was the age of the patient. Infants and children were most commonly burned by hot liquid spills. For example, a child would inadvertently grasp the handle of a pot of hot fluids, spilling it onto himself. The misuse of liquid accelerants, like gasoline, was the precipitating factor for most burn injuries in adolescents and adults. Because we had now identified the age-specific causal factor of burn injuries, we have tried valiantly to institute public educational campaigns using television public service announcements that alerted families to these preventable burn injuries.

Our scientific studies on burn care allowed us to bring scientific advances to the burn patient's bedside. Even though we were developing new products for burn care, we lacked a separate burn treatment facility with specially trained staff to care for these challenging patients. Consequently, we were outspoken advocates for developing a separate burn treatment facility. I am saddened that our plans for building a burn center were not rapidly implemented. After completing architectural designs for a burn center over a 10-year period, hospital administrators informed me that they did not have adequate funds for this new facility. Hearing this news, I went immediately to the Vice-President of the Health Sciences Center, Dr. Harry Muller, who had been a great advisor and friend. I explained to Dr. Muller that I had worked for 10 years to develop a burn center to care for these challenging patients. I had convinced hospital administration of the importance of this healthcare facility and they had promised to allocate money for its construction. I had now been told that there were no funds for this facility. My heart was broken. Dr. Muller comforted me by explaining, "The medical center cannot allow you to have a broken heart. For that reason alone, we will have a burn center." In these days of careful monitoring of expenditures, Dr. Muller's rationale for having a burn center, which was to fix my broken heart, today would obviously not be accepted by health planners. Because he was a cardiac surgeon, I believe that he had valid insight into correcting broken hearts. In any event, a new burn center was erected.

Chronic Wounds and Pressure Ulcers

In 1995, Dr. Rodeheaver and I championed another major improvement in the clinical care of chronic wounds and pressure sores, the development of a hyperbaric treatment center. This center exposes patients with wounds to elevated atmospheric pressures so their tissue is subjected to increased concentrations of oxygen. This treatment modality is very successful in treating wounds infected by organisms that live in the absence of oxygen, anaerobic organisms. Moreover, this clinical service has been expanded to treat patients with long-standing wounds that resist treatment. This program was a joint effort between Dr. Raymond Morgan, Professor and Chairman of the Department of Plastic Surgery, and Dr. Paul Levine, Chairman of the Department of Otolaryngology and Head and Neck Surgery. During the last two years, more than 250 patients have received treatment in this facility.

It will come as no surprise to you that one of our greatest challenges has been to raise sufficient research funds to support the innovative scientists in our laboratory. While research grants from the federal government and industry have been an important source of support, generous gifts from grateful patients and friends have allowed us to reach for the stars. I also must acknowledge my close friend, Maria Mike-Mayer, Director of the Texaco Foundation, who has provided grants to our burn center during the last 20 years. My successes in raising moneys for worthwhile research programs can be credited to lessons I learned from my mentor, Dr. Wangensteen. He felt that the best kept *profile for success* in fund-raising was timely personal communication with the donor. He reminded me that I must acknowledge the generous donor at the end of each published scientific paper and send a copy with a personal, handwritten note to each donor.

As I look to the future of our medical center, I believe the University must position itself in the center of scientific achievements by creating a unique alliance between University and private industry. Drs. Rodeheaver, Thacker and I can attest to the fact that this alliance provides invaluable benefits to industry as well as the University. These benefits include additional support for academic health centers, the potential for increased scientific and commercial productivity in both spheres and enhancement of the educational experiences of students and fellows.

The University of Virginia purchased the 525-acre North Fork property in 1987. This tract of land is located just north of Charlottesville in Virginia's historic Albemarle County. This property had been used as a cow pasture for eight years as it completely lacked in any infrastructure: no roads, sewer, or power. Drs. Rodeheaver, Thacker and I attracted the first tenant of the North Fork Research Park, MicroAire Surgical Instru-

Prescription for Teaching

The teacher must make room for the voice of the inner child within each of us so that we can feel genuine and creative.

Alice Miller[12] spoke of a fool who threw a stone into the water and believed that a hundred sages could bring it back. A child would quickly realize the futility of the sages' meaningless attempts to recover this worthless stone. She felt that this was a perfect reflection of the despair of a bright child in the face of the stupidity of "mature" adults. She pointed out that a child genius who still thinks in pictures might be justifiably puzzled by the sages' efforts to recover the lost stone. The child might ask the question, "Isn't the world full of stones? Why should a hundred clever people try so hard to get this one back? Why don't they look around? If they do, they may find all kinds of new treasure they can't see because they are so busy searching in vain in the water!"

Our students must be treated as the princes and princesses of possibility and must be in an environment friendly to learning.

In the lively leaven of an atmosphere fostering inquiry, no one must be afraid to come forward with a novel idea, no matter how strange or unfamiliar it may sound.

Teachers must invite their students to join them on creative journeys that can produce positive changes in the world.

Teachers can present puzzling questions to their students that will transform the student's perceptions of apparently impossible problems into opportunities for solution.

The teacher must stir the student's imagination to provide new energy and insight into unsolved mysteries and to answer questions about our lives.

As a teacher and student's minds join together in new explorations, there will be an intellectual fusion and transformation in which the student becomes the teacher. Young students are so eager to learn, so ardent in their desire to make their contributions to the fostering of knowledge, that all a teacher does is provide them with the opportunity and not stand in their way.

Sufficient financial resources must be available to allow students to achieve their dreams.

The financial needs of student, residents, fellows, and faculty vary considerably and are unpredictable. I have always tried to assist them so they can have sufficient moneys for food, shelter, clothing, and healthcare to ensure their survival. Educational support for books, computers, and journals opens new horizons. Moneys for travel to educational conferences and other universities add an important dimension to their lives. A gift of a favorite painting serves as a constant reminder of our friendship as they seek to inherit eternity.

Each of us has many potential selves. It is within the power of most of us to decide what manner of person and physician we shall be.

In his inaugural presidential speech in 1994, Nelson Mandella eloquently spoke about this unique beauty and brilliance of people who transform followers into leaders: "Our deepest fear is not that we are inadequate. Our deepest fear is that we are powerful beyond measure. It is our light, not our darkness, that most frightens us. We ask ourselves, 'Who am I to be brilliant, gorgeous, talented, and fabulous?' Actually, who are you not to be? You are a child of God. Your playing small doesn't serve the world. There is nothing enlightened about shrinking so that other people won't feel insecure around you. We were born to make manifest the glory of God that is within us. It's not just in some of us; it's in everyone. And if we let our own light shine, we unconsciously give other people permission to do the same. As we are liberated from our own fear, our presence automatically liberates others."

ments, Inc. (MSI). In mid-1978, the Marmon Group acquired this company who developed the first line of sterile packaged disposable blades, drills and burrs for small bone surgery. It now offers more than 1,000 different accessories for powered surgical instruments for all makers and manufactures the largest selection of powered surgical tools worldwide.

MSI's move to Charlottesville is a dream come true for MSI as well as the university. Several surgical departments have developed collaborative research programs that are resulting in important surgical advances. In addition, graduate students are being hired by MSI to strengthen their company. The walls separating the University from industry are crumbling, allowing the development of a new, empowered academic village that is preparing us for the 21st century. I can attest that the University of Virginia is very interested in attracting biotechnology companies to the North Fork Research Park. Your visit to MicroAire Surgical Instruments, Inc. at 1641 Edlich Drive will demonstrate the unique opportunities in our developing alliance between the University and industry.

As I continue my scientific journey in Virginia, I remain committed to the concept of developing an academic village that is friendly to learning. I would like my students to remember that they come into medical school with childlike dreams and visions of improving the lives of their patients, developing new cures for diseases and sharing their expertise with their progeny. I do remember how the medical information overload delivered by thousands of lectures, handout sheets, books and the endless hours of cramming facts into one's mind can diminish such dreams and visions. The grading system that ranks students in relation to one another reinforces a developing cynicism toward their future in medicine. Testing has pitted students against faculty when the student views the faculty member as someone to be manipulated for a good grade, rather than a trusted ally.

My greatest fear is that our students might allow the ineptness of our educational system to transform their loving commitment to scientific excellence and inquiry into materialistic and self-serving values. If I could do but one thing for them, I would choose to reinspire, rejuvenate and revitalize their dreams of what physicians and medical scientists can be. They must realize that they must be *present in the moment* with their patients and that these interactions will become a *life-defining experience*. They must view the patient's catastrophic illness as *a life transforming opportunity* to solve the patient's problem. Moreover, they must enthusiastically enlist the help of other scientists and encourage them to become *powerful problem-solvers* for the patient. Armed with one victory over illness, they must change this one salvation into a *societal transformation program* for other patients. As adventurers become consumed by the journey, they must balance their life with joyful personal experiences that allow them to smell the roses.

I know that all the secrets and enigmas of medical sciences will be answered from uninhibited dreams. The marvelous reward for carrying into later life the ability to dream is that the opportunity to transform a dream into a meaningful solution will increase dramatically as one's wisdom and ingenuity develop. What I wish for my students more than anything else is that they may continue their childlike dreams of medical advances. It is the best assurance that they will never be one of those diffident and fearful souls who have known neither victory nor defeat.

In the following prescription for teaching, I have distilled the many pearls of thoughtful wisdom bestowed on me by Dr. Wangensteen. While his arena was surgery, he was the quintessential teacher from whose story all of us can learn valuable lessons. After all, we are all teachers.

4

Healers' Adventure

"The subject of healing stretches beyond medicine into issues about what we value in society and who we are as human beings. As patients, we are more than lonely, isolated flecks of matter; we are members of families, communities, and cultures. As this awareness finds its way into hospitals, operating rooms, clinics, and doctor's offices, perhaps it will spread further, as well. Healing begins with caring. So does civilization."

Bill Moyers

During my medical school training as well as surgical residency, I began to see that the provision of medical care to a patient was episodic, involving a given span of time and only one physician. As a *healer*, I would work independently until I found resolution to the problem. If I did not have the expertise, I would seek the advice of physicians who did. The documented outcome of my prescribed treatment was based solely on the patients' response to therapy.

After being faced with the real-life drama of serious illness and injury, I realized that healing was a team effort involving a wide variety of health professionals that included physicians. Moreover, the success of our team effort was often based on the time it took to provide treatment of the seriously injured patient. Response time became one of the most important outcome measures used to determine the efficiency of the team. Consequently, my view of healing changed dramatically from an isolated, physician–oriented therapeutic event to a coordinated system of care involving many health professionals from the time of injury until complete rehabilitation. You would think that, when faced with life-threatening illness or traumatic injury, physicians would champion this systematic approach to emergency care.

In the 1960s, physicians were, in fact, reluctant to develop such a coordinated approach. At that time, the emergency response to the injured soldier on the battlefield was far superior to that of, for example, the automobile accident victim in this country. Today, this emergency system is in place and has saved thousands of lives. The implementation, however, was an adventure filled with conflict and hostility precipitated by physicians' fear of losing control, stature and finally, money.

Dr. Wangensteen would not be surprised by this resistance to change. In my frequent meetings with Dr. Wangensteen, he often cautioned me that the road toward success can be a tortuous and dangerous pathway. He indicated that opposition would arise that would provide eloquent and disarming reasons for abandoning my dreams. Smiling, he would remind me that the magnitude of the opposition would often be proportionate to the merits of the *goals*. He warned me that the zeal of my opponents might be sufficient to kill the messenger, as well as the message.

When I reflect on the origin of our comprehensive emergency medical system in the United States, Dr. Wangensteen's prophetic comments on the *Profiles for Success* and survival are readily apparent. During the last 30 years, we have witnessed profound changes in emergency care of the sick and injured. One of the highlights was the adventures undertaken by three healers in their development of a modern emergency medical system.[1]

Drs. James Mills, R A. Cowley, and David Boyd were, in large part, responsible for the emergence of the specialty of emergency medicine, the development of the modern university trauma center, and the establishment of a nationwide emergency medical service system. Our nationwide emergency medical system stands as witness to their enduring influence on the delivery of emergency care. The results of their efforts are most apparent in the improved care of patients with life-threatening illnesses or injuries.

Emergence of the Specialty of Emergency Medicine

James Mills' training and experience prepared him for a leadership role in medicine. He served as a line officer in the Navy for four years (1941–1945) during World War II before entering medical school at the Washington University. His military service to our country became a *life-defining experience*. His additional three years of service in the Navy as a physician (1950–1953) showed him an organized approach to emer-

Dr. James Mills defined the education, role, and responsibility of the emergency department physician.

gency care that was not available to the injured civilian, confirming that the chances for survival would be better in a combat zone than on the average city street. Because the military had a coordinated system of emergency care, he watched how skilled emergency medical teams changed a catastrophic injury into a *life-transforming opportunity*. After leaving the Navy at age 36, he started a practice in family medicine in Alexandria, Virginia, and was very involved in community service, becoming a member of the Board of Directors of Alexandria Community Health Center in 1956, a position he held for the next 18 years.

Within seven years after starting his practice, Jim was a recognized medical leader. He was elected President of the Medical Staff of Alexandria Hospital in 1961, which provided him with a unique overview of the entire hospital's healthcare delivery system. The dissatisfaction expressed by the patients treated in the hospital's emergency room caught his attention. "The public has come to look upon the emergency department as the community medical center where any man may apply with any complaint, at any hour of the day or night, and expect prompt and courteous attention his due." His emergency department was staffed by interns, residents, and nurses, with the backing of the attending staff. As attrition of the resident staff developed in his hospital, efforts were made to supplant this service. "One solution was to call the medical staff to serve in rotation. This was met with less than enthusiasm by doctors who had put in more than 60 hours a week in our practice." Jim then identified a *goal* that would solve this healthcare crisis: *staff emergency departments with physicians trained and credentialed in emergency medicine.* Jim devised a revolutionary physician staffing plan to meet the patients' needs in his emergency department, which marked the beginning of modern emergency medicine. Jim enlisted the help of three *powerful problem-solvers* who would make a revolutionary change in medicine. He and three of his physician colleagues, actively engaged in private practice, agreed to relinquish their practice and become *full-time* emergency department physicians. His managerial skills were evident in his selection of the medical staff. He recruited physicians in family medicine who were respected as doctors, who had taken on leadership roles in the hospital, and who were his close personal friends. It is remarkable that these pioneers in emergency medicine, Jim Mills, John McDade, Chalmers Loughridge, and William Weaver, remained together in emergency medical practice for their entire professional careers.

In 1963, Jim reported the 15 months' experience of his Alexandria plan in the *Virginia Medical Monthly*.[2] He indicated that, "The doctors of the emergency department continue to enjoy the cordial relations with their confreres they had in private practice. The staff members of the several services have been most helpful in their essential backing of the emergency department. The doctors of the community have learned that the service can help them with their patients during busy office hours, evenings off, or nights, with the assurance that their own doctor-patient relationship will be preserved . . . the 12-month patient load has increased 14% over the previous year." When the American Medical Association highlighted the Alexandria plan in their news, national attention focused on this new health professional, the full-time emergency medical physician. His innovation was a giant step ahead of the previous staffing either with interns and residents or rotating staff members of the attending staff.

With the need for around-the-clock skilled professional care demonstrated, the next step in its evolution was obvious to Jim Mills: the specialized training of physicians whose career choice was in emergency medicine. The dream of Jim and his talented Alexandria emergency physician colleagues was expanded to develop a *societal transformation program* that would allow patients in other hospitals to gain the same benefit of experienced care in the emergency department as encountered in Alexandria, Virginia. By 1978, as result of his pioneering efforts, 30 university programs offered formal residency training programs in emergency medicine. The graduates of these programs entered active practice of emergency medicine and were in great demand to upgrade the quality of emergency service. At this time, Jim Mills accepted a leadership role in the American College of Emergency Physicians to develop a specialty certification "which will designate those men and women having demonstrated by training and examination that they qualify as certified emergency physicians specialists." As president of the organization from 1971 to 1973, Jim Mills championed the development of certifying boards in emergency medicine. He served on the Board of Directors from 1976 until 1988, and was appointed as President of the Board in 1986. Within 28 years, Jim Mills was able to realize his professional dream: a modern emergency department whose certified and well-trained emergency physicians expeditiously and effectively treated their patients with courtesy and compassion.

Jim Mills was a visionary, a *powerful problem-solver*, and he was willing to take the risk if he thought the gain would be worth it. He planted the seed from which a new specialty grew. On April 25, 1989, he succumbed to an unusually aggressive myelogenous leukemia, leaving the specialty of emergency medicine as a legacy for us all.

Modern University Trauma Centers

R Adams Cowley, the founder of the first modern university trauma center, was born in Layton, Utah, in 1917. One detail of Cowley's personal life deserves mention. When the complete name of R Adams Cowley is used, the omission of a period after the "R" is no accident. His father, Rufus Adams, a forceful gentleman of the tradition of the Mormon school, insisted that the baby boy be named after him. His wife pointed out that Rufus was such an awful name that even the father himself signed with an initial only. She compromised by writing the initial "R" on the birth certificate without a period. His name evolved into the nickname "R A."

Dr. R A. Cowley, founder of the first modern emergency trauma center.

R A. pursued his undergraduate studies at the University of Utah in Salt Lake City (1936–1940), after which he elected to continue his education at the University of Maryland School of Medicine (1940–1944). He worked his way though college and medical school, while struggling to support his family. His surgical residency began in 1945 at the University of Maryland and was interrupted in 1946 by military service, which had considerable influence on his surgical career. As Chief of Surgery for a field hospital, he was sent to Europe soon after World War II ended. Like Jim Mills, R A.'s military service became a *life-defining experience*. He soon discovered that there was abundance of surgical opportunity in the war's aftermath with civilians being assaulted and injured throughout Europe. In 1946, he worked under virtual wartime conditions in the operating rooms of his hospital in Mourmalon, France. As he gained experience, he became Chief of General Surgery of the 98th General Hospital in Munich, Germany. R A. repeatedly witnessed the military emergency medical system's ability to change a catastrophic

accidental injury into a *life-transforming opportunity*. Cowley acknowledged his debt to the army, which had introduced him to the field of
trauma, a subject that would be the focus of his entire professional career
at the University of Maryland where he became a skilled cardiothoracic
surgeon.

Later, when he joined the faculty at the University of Maryland, open
heart surgery had become an established field that attracted the attention
of most cardiothoracic surgeons. With the memories of his military experience fresh in his mind, however, he embarked on his 40-year odyssey in
trauma care. He saw a sharp contrast between trauma care in the military
and that provided in hospitals in the United States. In the military, he
knew that all trauma victims were treated by a trained shock trauma unit.
In civilian hospitals, most trauma patients rarely received care in a shock
trauma unit. In reflecting on his early career after leaving the military,
Cowley commented: "The God's truth is that most emergency rooms are
awful. I get into trouble every time I say that and some miserable son of a
bitch quotes me in the newspaper, but it's true. Even today you live or die
depending on where you have your accident, because in most places they
take you to the nearest hospital." R A. had clearly identified a *goal* for his
life, "*I want to save the lives of injured Americans.*"

His concepts of trauma care began in the mid-1950s when his studies
of shock in animals demonstrated the importance of immediate care.[3] He
focused on the trauma patient who had lost blood, suffering an extreme
drop in blood pressure. When he took a quart of blood from a laboratory
dog, Cowley caused the animal to develop shock. By returning the blood
to the animal quickly, the animal would recover. If the animal remained
in shock more than one hour, "the golden hour," death came slowly to all
dogs. Dr. Cowley had developed a simple but revolutionary concept: he
related the duration of shock directly to life expectancy. Consequently,
he concluded the trauma team must restore the patients' blood pressure
within that golden hour to save patients' lives.

His early clinical studies of shock in the trauma patient were funded
by an Army Research Development Contract, which later supported the
development of his two-room Clinical Shock Trauma Research Unit in
1961. Skeptics referred to it as the "death lab." After a trauma patient
died, Cowley's residents searched for new patients to enter the unit: "We
were the black birds of the hospital, man," commented Dr. David Boyd,
one of Cowley's star residents. "Whenever we showed up on the wards,
the nurse would dive for their charts to see who was in shock. Whenever

we were around, someone was dying." David Boyd's care of the civilian trauma patient became a *life-defining experience* that would have considerable impact on emergency care in our country. When a prospective patient was located, the doctor was often very supportive of transferring the patient to the death lab. Death with dignity was still an unrecognized concept and the family was usually begging the physician to do anything. From the beginning, half the patients brought to the death lab did not die. These results made Cowley ecstatic. He realized the potential impact of the 50,000 people who were dying on highways each year, more than 800 in his own state of Maryland. If he had a big enough trauma center, he knew he could save at least half of these lives.

The trauma unit, with the backing of the National Institutes of Health and the State of Maryland, grew into the first modern Shock Trauma Center for the study of trauma. His trauma unit was new, bright – and remained empty because community physicians refused to refer patients to Cowley. Many physicians who potentially could refer patients felt threatened because they viewed him as an empire-builder who wanted to steal their patients.

The most recent impetus to develop trauma centers has been to designate and isolate a few beds in the emergency room or in an intensive care unit (ICU) and call it a trauma center. The space allocation rarely resulted in fundamental changes in the care given in the emergency room or ICU. R A. realized that the mission of the emergency departments and the ICUs were different than that of a true trauma center. The emergency department must be geared to a wide variety of patients with different conditions, most of which are *not* life-threatening. In contrast, the ICU was structured around the in-hospital transferred patient, already diagnosed and treated, who required more intensive care.

Consequently, his trauma center was neither an emergency department nor an ICU. His trauma center had a first contact area, combining the best of the emergency department and the ICU, always prepared to immediately admit and treat the most critically ill and injured patients. "Unlike the ICU, the trauma patient arrives undiagnosed and untreated with his survival at stake." His center had the ability to provide resuscitation as well as diagnostic and therapeutic measures for the most critical situations, and they continued such care until that patient's condition stabilized. R A.'s cardinal rule was "treatment before diagnosis."

In his center, all necessary lifesaving services, diagnostic and ancillary, revolved around the patient. Treatment was immediate, and operations were performed on instant notice. Rehabilitative measures began on admission and were a fundamental, continuous part of care to minimize disability. In his trauma center, there was no waiting. Resuscitation, stabilization, definitive care, and rehabilitation were all a part of his trauma center, and they all began on admission.

As his clinical expertise to manage those patients became established, R A. still had to enlist the help of *powerful problem-solvers* who would devise a transportation and communication system that would safely bring patients to his trauma center. Working with the Maryland State Police Aviation Division, he developed an efficient and cost-effective Air Med-Evac Helicopter Program. Helicopters were based across the state, and the patients were flown directly to the trauma facility in Baltimore from almost any corner of the state in less than one hour, the golden hour for treating the trauma patient. Simultaneously, a communication network grew to coordinate Med-Evac transport and to notify the receiving facility. That basic system was expanded so that Maryland had the first comprehensive statewide communication system to provide radio contact between the scene of an emergency, ambulances, hospitals, specialty referral centers, Med-Evac helicopters, and fire department central alarms, with both voice and telemetry capabilities. Cowley's growing emergency medical system won support from the State and the University, and after reorganization in 1973, became an autonomous Institute within the University of Maryland. This Institute combined the Shock Trauma Center with the statewide Emergency Medical System program.

The development of his modern trauma center within a university setting was not accomplished without difficulties. Resistance to a physically and administratively separate facility was intense. He also had to overcome opposition of healthcare professionals and administrators who were reluctant to relinquish control over the trauma center. R A. surmounted these enormous obstacles and demonstrated the significant potential of a modern trauma center in a university setting that had reached the *goals* of excellence of care at all levels, standards of therapy developed through research and education, dissemination of new knowledge, and provision of care systems for the community.

On the morning of April 13, 1971, the tide of resistance dramatically changed when then-Governor Marvin Mandel was fortuitously involved in trauma care.[3] When his long-time friend, James P. Mause, House Clerk, was involved in a serious auto accident, the ambulance took him to a nearby hospital in Frederick, Maryland. Because the doctors at the hospitals were unable to care for his injuries, he was referred to a larger facility in nearby Hagerstown. When Mandel was alerted to the severity of his friend's injuries, he immediately intervened by sending a state police helicopter with a trained medic to transfer him to the trauma unit at the University of Maryland. Governor Mandel went immediately to the unit and remembers distinctly his meeting with his seriously ill friend. He indicated to Mandel that he wanted a pad and pencil. With considerable effort, Mause wrote: "Marvin, please, I want to live." Immediately after their meeting, Cowley took Mause to the operating room for emergency surgery. Cowley's team saved Mause's life. Cowley then took the governor on a tour of the Shocktrauma facility. Realizing the enormous benefit of the center, the governor become a strong advocate for Cowley.

Despite Cowley's clinical achievements in the care of the trauma patient, there was still continued resistance to patient transfer as well as criticism of Cowley's efforts. When this criticism wended its way to the Governor's office, Mandel commented: "I think medical politics are much tougher than politics as I know it. Much tougher. They tried to make Dr. Cowley look like an individual who'd gone berserk, who was doing everything counter to what the medical profession would want to see. And, oh, my God, they had meetings all over the place, denouncing him."

When the autonomy of the Shocktrauma center was threatened by the Chairman of the Department of Surgery at the University of Maryland, Governor Mandel interceded and signed an executive order that created the Maryland Institute for Emergency Medical Services and separated the trauma unit from the Department of Surgery. With the skillful use of his friendship with Mandel, Cowley sold the concept of the Shocktrauma center to the state of Maryland. He had successfully affected a *societal transformation program* that would allow all patients in Maryland to gain the benefit of care in a modern trauma center. Ultimately, he directed the entire emergency medical system of Maryland as well as a new $50 million, 7-story, 138-bed trauma center until his retirement in 1989. Most physicians are convinced that he is the most successful trauma surgeon in the world, an achievement that was recognized appropriately by naming the new modern trauma center the R Adams Cowley Shock Trauma Center. R Adams Cowley died October 27, 1991, of heart failure at the age of 74. This giant of trauma care was buried with military honors at Arlington National Cemetery.

Development of Nationwide Emergency Medical Services Systems

David Boyd was born in 1937 and grew up in Seattle where his father coordinated and implemented physical education programs for the city's playgrounds. What influence his father's charismatic managerial skills had on Dave's career is uncertain, but it provided an atmosphere in which young individuals were fulfilling many of their athletic and personal dreams. Dave's heart was set on a career in medicine, and he pursued his medical school studies at Magill University in Montreal. Dr. Jan Langman, Professor of Anatomy at Magill, recognized Dave as a gifted student who was bright, personable, and energetic and destined to be a great academic surgeon. Perceiving distinct limitations in the clinical experience at Magill University, Dave selected an internship at Cook

Dr. David R. Boyd was responsible for developing a system for emergency medical services throughout the nation.

County Hospital in Chicago, which was deluged by an enormous number of challenging patients.

It is fortuitous that his postgraduate educational program was interrupted by two years of military service. He was stationed in Baltimore, Maryland, in proximity to R Adams Cowley who was starting his Clinical Shock Trauma Research Unit at the University of Maryland. Cowley convinced Dave to take a fellowship there. This fellowship was the beginning of a *life-defining experience* for Dave in which he saw the development of R A.'s embryonic modern trauma center that was saving the lives of seriously injured persons who were destined to die. He developed a close personal friendship with RA. that spanned both their professional careers. Because the beds in R A.'s trauma unit were frequently empty, Dave became impatient and frustrated, wanting more experience with seriously ill patients. Consequently, Dave returned to the Cook County Hospital hoping to further enhance his clinical experience.

While fulfilling his surgical clinical residency responsibilities, Dave focused considerable attention on the entire system of shock trauma, from the time of injury to rehabilitation. In the fourth year of his residency, he was the recipient of a National Institutes of Health grant to develop a computerized trauma registry that would evaluate the outcomes of such care. His successful application to the National Institutes of Health, in which he served as a principal investigator, was a unique accomplishment for a surgical resident. With the rigid peer-review process for such grants, faculty members, rather than a resident, are usually the only successful applicants.

Dave was making progress, but he dreamed of an organized approach for treating the trauma patient. Working with Dr. Bruce Flashner, Assistant to the Coordinator for Health Services in Illinois, they drafted a proposal for an organized approach that would serve as a starting point for a state health plan on emergency services. On December 16, 1970, Governor Richard Ogilvie approved this plan and enlisted Dave's help to develop Illinois' emergency medical service system. His appointment as director of the Illinois emergency medical system was a *life-transforming opportunity* to devise a system of emergency medical care that would save lives throughout the state.

Dave's surgical mentors at Cook County Hospital encouraged him to accept this position, but only as part-time employment, so he could pursue his promising academic surgical career at Cook County Hospital. They cautioned him that acceptance of a full-time administrative position would probably end his academic surgical career. After careful consideration and fully appreciating the significant potential consequences of his decision, he resigned his academic affiliations to ensure that he would have an objective view of the Illinois Health care system that was not constrained by the ambitions of any health care facility. He became the full-time director of Emergency Health Services in the Illinois Department of Health in 1971.

His achievements in Illinois were facilitated by his successful application to the Department of Health, Education and Welfare for an Emergency Medical Service demonstration project.[4] Dave championed the development of a coordinated program in trauma care in Illinois, which served as a model for coordinated burn care and spinal cord treatment for the nation. At that point in his life, he identified his *goal: development of an effective emergency medical system in our nation.* If David was going to implement a nationwide emergency medical system, he would have to enlist the help of *powerful problem-solvers* in the federal government, Congress and the President of the United States. His accomplishments in Illinois received national recognition and made him the ideal candidate to head the Division of Emergency Medical Services of the Department of Health, Education and Welfare. The department was preparing to implement the Emergency Service Systems Act in 1973, which for the first time provided mechanisms and funds for communities across the nation. With passage of this Act, Congress mandated that the emergency medical care programs funded with federal assistance must address, plan, and implement, a "systems" approach for the provision of emergency response and medical care. This legislation established emergency medical services as a national health problem, identified the lead agency as the Division of Emergency Medical Services of the Department of Health, Education and Welfare, and prescribed the 15 essential components necessary to establish an effective systems approach to care on a regional basis.

During his 10 years as Director of the Division of Emergency Medical Services of the Department of Health, Education and Welfare, Dave was responsible for assisting and developing emergency medical service systems throughout the nation and for distributing approximately $185 million in grant funds among the 50 states, major urban health departments, and some 303 geographically contiguous regional emergency medical service programs. He supervised a national and diverse program staff of more than 100 people and was responsible for initiating programs involving virtually every hospital and emergency service provider in a variety of ways, including the designation of more than 1,000 trauma centers, 300 burn centers, 100 spinal cord treatment centers and 600 poison control centers. He was instrumental in upgrading hospitals to higher levels of emergency care through processes of classification, categorization and designation, and through a variety of educational activities. Although there were numerous and varied emergent conditions, he established that six critical target patient areas would be identified in regional emergency medical service systems planning: major accidental trauma, burn injuries, spinal cord injuries, heart attacks, poisonings, high-risk infants and mothers, and behavioral and psychiatric emergencies. Through this regional approach to emergency care, the initial and definitive medical care for each target patient group was improved. Many of these patients were saved by the developing emergency medical system in our country.

Another remarkable aspect of his national emergency medical service experience has been the leadership and participatory role of governmental organized medicine at all levels. The Emergency Medical Systems Act in 1973 was, in fact, one of the first pieces of health legislation supported by organized medicine, as were its amendments in 1976 and 1979. Traditional antigovernmental opposition often espoused by the medical profession and the public did not appear; in fact, many from these sectors actively and willingly participated in a cooperative way, working with governmental interests in establishing emergency medical services systems programs and their activities. Through Dave's leadership, the 1970s witnessed an almost explosive *societal transformation program* in the conceptual design, planning, and implementation of emergency medical services in our nation. Dave spent the most productive years of his professional career in the relentless pursuit of a *goal* he realized: the genesis of a nationwide comprehensive organized emergency medical service system. There was another notable aspect of this governmentally subsidized plan to improve emergency medical services. When the period of government assistance ended and the funds were depleted, the federal government ended its involvement in planning and coordinating emergency medical care on a national level and delegated this responsibility to each state. This termination of funding did not end improvements in emergency medicine because an infrastructure had been developed in each state that allowed them to initiate continued cost-effective innovations in emergency care. In my experience, the successful transformation of a federal responsibility to a state initiative has rarely been accomplished, resulting in a massive federal bureaucracy that has become fiscally unmanageable and irresponsible.

In 1996, the University of Virginia Health Sciences Center established the annual David R. Boyd Lectureship in Emergency Medical Systems and Trauma care to provide an international forum to document recent advances in these fields. The first Boyd lecture was held at the University of Virginia on March 22, 1997. Dr. Marcus L. Martin, Professor and Chairman of the Department of Emergency Medicine at the University of Virginia Health Sciences Center, acknowledged Dr. Boyd at this conference by the following comment: "Rarely can a major medical advancement and societal change be attributed to one person. However, the Trauma and Emergency Medical Services (Trauma/EMS) Systems that now provide ubiquitous access and prompt delivery of sophisticated field and organized hospital care for every U.S. citizen are the direct result of the lifetime contribution of Dr. David R. Boyd. He is recognized as the physician/citizen who, in the early 1970's identified the obvious deficiencies and lack of systemization in emergency care, initially for trauma victims and subsequently for all types of medical conditions."

These *healers*, working primarily outside of the university academic environment, designed a system of healthcare that has saved thousands of lives. These individuals were skilled physicians who approached emergency care from different perspectives with the same ultimate *goal* in mind, saving the patient's life. In Alexandria, Virginia, Jim Mills saw the need for full-time trained emergency physicians who provided care to patients in a specialized facility of the hospital, the emergency department. He envisioned and empowered the development of residency training programs in emergency medicine that allowed them to be credentialed in this specialty. Working in nearby Baltimore, R A. Cowley focused on the critical care of the trauma patient who necessitated life-saving treatments within a prescribed period of time, "the golden hour." Because this treatment had to begin from the time of injury, he orchestrated a statewide system of healthcare that would bring the critically ill patient to his comprehensive treatment center, the Shocktrauma Center. David Boyd expanded Cowley's approach to trauma care to a nationwide system and pursued the development of his concepts, plans, and programs from his home state of Illinois to the White House and Congress. During his ten years as Director of the Division of Emergency Medical Services of the Department of Health, Education, and Welfare, Dr. Boyd was responsible for developing EMS systems throughout the nation.

5

Disciple's Expedition

"Cure the patient as well as the disease."
Dr. Alvin Barach

I accepted the position of Acting Director of the Emergency Medical Services at the University of Virginia Health Sciences Center in 1974. I would like to first enumerate my specialized clinical and educational emergency healthcare experiences that allowed me to be selected for this position: none. I had no formal training in prehospital care, emergency care, or trauma care. The fact is there were no other applicants for this position when my predecessor resigned. Because I had extensive experience in general surgery, plastic surgery, and research, the University was worried that my academic credentials would cause me to focus more on research than clinical care. By appointing me Acting Director, the University was implying that I could be easily terminated from the position if I did not fulfill responsibilities that were never actually defined. During the next 12 years, my academic title was never changed from Acting Director to Director because the University was continually concerned that I was making too many changes in the emergency room (ER).

On my first day as Acting Director, I thought it would be appropriate to gather together the entire staff involved in caring for the nearly 35,000 patients treated annually in the ER. The staff consisted of second-year surgical residents, third-year medical residents, full-time emergency medical nurses, and one hospital administrator. I had no supervisory control over the staff because these individuals reported to their own administrative department heads.

I scheduled a meeting with this wide range of health professionals who treated this large number of patients, personally contacted each of the individuals and posted announcements of our first conference. I anticipated participating in a dynamic conference in which we would share visions about the future of the ER. When I arrived at 8 a.m. for the conference, I was surprised that no one was there. After waiting for 15 minutes in the empty room, I set out to find out why no one showed up. The medical and surgical residents were sleeping because they had been awake all night taking care of patients. The nursing staff was busy preparing for a change in shift. The hospital administrator could not be found.

After receiving this warm reception, I immediately reflected on the sage advice of Dr. Wangensteen regarding selecting a field in medicine. He had reminded me that there are two important considerations. First, select a field that is important to humankind and that provides an opportunity to save lives. Second, choose a field in which relatively few health professionals see opportunities for revolutionary advances in care. It would appear that the directorship of the University of Virginia Emergency Medical Services had met all of his criteria for an ideal job. Armed with his wise advice, I learned the ropes by using a system of crisis management.

With regard to our prehospital system, I found that most rescue squads were poorly trained and driving antiquated vehicles with no radio communication system. In 1974, the minimum requirements for certification of ambulance attendants was the American Red Cross Advanced First Aid Course, which was generally considered inadequate for those who were required to render care to persons who were seriously ill. Most rescue vehicles had citizen band radios that allowed them to communicate to the University police who would relay the message to the ER by telephone. As I prepared for my first transport of an accident victim to the ER, I was surprised to find a patient who had been injured in an automobile accident, was not breathing, but resting comfortably on a soft stretcher. The 42-year-old male patient had cold, purplish-colored skin and no detectable vital signs. He must have been dead for at least 30 minutes. When I asked the rescue squad if they had performed cardiopulmonary resuscitation (CPR), they indicated that they had no training in this technique. It was even more disturbing to find that none of the hospital personnel in the entire facility had any formal training in CPR. Consequently, they were ill-prepared to continue any lifesaving efforts they had started. I must acknowledge, however, that the nursing and administrative staff had an expeditious and organized plan to transfer the patient to the morgue. They knew exactly how to encircle the large toe of the corpse with a label, allowing proper identification and transfer to the funeral home. I must confess that I was horrified by the community and our hospital's emergency medical system. We had no life saving capability and served merely to transport the dead patient to the hospital. These memories caused me many sleepless nights and became my first *life-defining experience* in emergency medicine.

This was only the first of many frightening *life-defining experiences* involving other emergency clinical care services offered by our hospital. Let me try to accurately draw a picture of my painful memories. My reflections of these services are best illustrated by recounting several tragic and potentially preventable personal losses. In our crisis intervention service, a medical resident had answered a telephone call from a patient who was threatening to kill himself. The suicidal patient had organized a detailed plan, ensuring that he would be successful in his effort. He told the resident that he had placed a microphone next to his heart so that he could localize the audible noises of his heartbeat to ensure an accurate shot from his gun. The resident pleaded with him not to take this desperate action and offered to get immediate psychiatric consultation. After carefully writing down the patient's name and telephone number, he immediately called the psychiatric resident, asking him to contact the suicidal patient. The psychiatric resident, who was busy interviewing a patient who was to be admitted to his service, delayed returning the call for at least five minutes. His delayed call to the patient was not answered. Forty-five minutes later, we received a call from the University police warning us that a rescue squad was bringing in this same patient with a self-inflicted bullet wound to his heart. Our emergency room staff had failed to save this frightened patient's life. This warning gave the nurses ample time to find another toe tag. The patient was dead on arrival and expeditiously transferred to the morgue.

Prior to 1976, our poison control system consisted of a drug card file that was updated daily by one of the clinical departments. A resident had received a telephone call indicating that a 4-year-old child had unwittingly swallowed 25 tablets of Tylenol®. He immediately called the pharmacy asking them for drug dose study to determine the risk to the child. The pharmacy immediately called back, indicating that this dosage of Tylenol® was potentially life-threatening, and recommended bringing the child immediately to the ER for treatment. The embarrassed resident was unable to contact the patient's family because he had not written down a name or phone number.

Sexual assault patients were being routinely interviewed in the hallway of the ER, preventing patient confidentiality. We had no guidelines for patient care or physical evidence recovery kits. Psychosocial support of the distressed individual was not provided by our staff. I had the perception that the distressed patient who was sexually assaulted was treated in the same cavalier manner as a college student complaining of a toothache. This deplorable medical care was a nauseating experience; the administrative staff and young residents were anaesthetized to the plight of the sexually abused.

Handwritten medical records were completed only by physicians who ignored the nurses' notes stapled to the back of the patients' medical records. Critical patient information provided by the nurses about a patient were lost in this confused system of care. After reading my description of care given to patients, the reader might reasonably argue that the patients should not pay for their clinical care. I soon learned that the inadequacy of our healthcare system in the ER was not the reason for the absence of a billing system. Receptionists did not have a computerized billing system and were not allowed to accept any cash payments. When I suggested the novel approach of billing patients for emergency medical services to the administrator, I was immediately reprimanded after he explained that the cost of this "free" care would be billed to the state government that would reimburse the University. Realizing the ineptitude of the infrastructure of the ER, I asked that my office in plastic surgery be relocated to the ER. Because the hospital had no funds for my relocation, they suggested I seek grant funds to pay for renovating my office.

As Acting Director of the Emergency Department, I inherited a clinical care system that ignored the illness or injury as well as the soul of the patient. This emergency healthcare system had to be reformed so that it treated and also listened to the heart of our patients. At the entrance to the ER, the staff had positioned a large, white board with each treatment room listed along the top of the board. A box outlined below the designated room was used for writing pertinent information regarding each patient. Patient identification was by illness or injury and may have included sexual assault. Chairs were positioned below the white board for patients who had not yet been interviewed, waiting to be escorted to the designated room. The white board was adjacent to the entrance of the ER so family and friends could have an effective overview of the challenging clinical problems. For the family and friends, it served as a news report, highlighting confidential information about neighbors and friends. This patient information board served as the lighted electric monitor in Times Square that updated society on all of the latest news.

I had my first glimmer of hope that a colleague or friend would join me in resuscitating our ER, as well as its emergency medical system, and would transform it into a dynamic and caring lifesaving system. It was as if God had sent an angel to my rescue. On a busy Saturday evening in 1975, one of our licensed practical nurses, Shirley Talbert, asked to speak to me privately regarding our care of sexual assault victims.[1] This conversation was another *life-defining experience* for me in which I was awakened to society's violence against both men and women. She spoke in a gentle and kind manner that did not reflect her exasperation with our incompetent care. She began by providing a simple overview of her concerns. "Dr. Edlich, our care of sexual assault victims in this ER is outdated, inappropriate, ineffective, and dangerous. We act as if we are in the dark ages of medical care. For instance, both the police and the physician interview sexual assault victims in the hallway. Moreover, we don't use an evidentiary recovery kit for obtaining legal specimens. Follow-up of these patients is nonexistent. I would recommend that we make some immediate changes." Because Shirley was so concerned , motivated, and knowledgeable about this subject, I asked her to head a sexual assault task force that would develop standard protocols. Moreover, I asked that she identify other interested nurses who would become familiar with her established treatment protocol. She pointed out that we were going to need considerable help from the police as well as attorneys to devise these protocols. She emphasized that the ER must have a demonstrated commitment to the care of these patients by allocating one treatment room to conduct confidential interviews with these patients as well as other assault victims. I agreed to her request and enlisted the help of our chief of police, John Bowen, as well as a dynamic attorney, Susan White. Both of these individuals helped organize protocols for the emergency care of the sexual assault victim, including guidelines for patient care, discussion of police investigations, written consent forms, and physical evidence recovery kits.

After developing these new protocols, I approached hospital administration regarding allocation of a separate room for confidential interviews. Because the space for our outdated ER was limited, there was an immediate reluctance to any space reallocation. After gaining consent from all departments in the hospital, I persuaded hospital administration

to reallocate this space. When this final decision was made, I did believe
that one of the administrators had severe misgivings about the new plan.
After the room was stripped of cabinets and shelves, the tile floors were
thoroughly cleaned in preparation for the change. My intuition about
hospital administration's reluctance to accept the changes was confirmed
when I asked the question, "Where can we get a couch and two chairs?"
The administrator responded, "We have no money available for furniture."

Fortunately, I was able to slowly make changes in the culture of the
ER and the hospital that allowed improvements in emergency care. We
had a new head nurse, Sue Loud, who was an emergency nurse practitioner. In addition, the hospital had hired a new director of nursing,
Helen Ripple, who was a champion for excellence in patient care. She
was a product of a devout Catholic family that was committed to service
to the disadvantaged. Because her brother is a talented plastic surgeon,
she became the sympathetic advocate of this young plastic surgeon who
wanted to improve emergency care. She had a new and innovative managerial style that allowed her to make immediate decisions. These decisions were based on her loving concern for patients in our hospital. When
I approached Helen regarding our sexual assault center without furniture, she had an immediate solution. Pointing at the furniture in her
office, she said, "Use any or all of the furniture in my office!" While
expressing my appreciation for her generous offer, I questioned her as to
how she planned to replace it. She responded, "Those folding metal
chairs in the hallway will be perfect."

The opening of our Crisis Center for Sexual Assault Victims had
numerous repercussions. First, the community was viewing the ER in a
new way, as a safe retreat for sexual assault victims in which they would
receive superb medical care that was coordinated with an effective legal
investigation. Shirley Talbert had expanded the nurse liaison role by
identifying a safe haven for the patient after discharge as well as being
present with the victim in any subsequent court appearances. This supportive environment for the sexual assault victim subsequently brought
victims out of the closet. Their numbers were so great that our nurse
liaison could no longer assume sole responsibility for their housing as
well as the other services she provided. Realizing the enormous magnitude of the problem, the community established a shelter for victims of
sexual assault and domestic violence. In addition, a non-profit organization with volunteer trained counselors was organized to serve as patient

advocates in the ER as well as following discharge from the hospital. Moreover, the legislation in Virginia was outdated and irresponsible and had to be changed to protect the sexual assault victim. It was blanketed with rules that protected the man against a "vengeful woman." Consequently, the victim was thoroughly cross-examined by the defendant's attorney about her past sexual activities. The victim had to prove that she resisted the rape to the utmost, despite threats to her life. Another feature of our antiquated rape legislation was the draconian penalties for the convicted assailant. Juries often acquitted, rather than send the defendant to prison for 20 or more years. Subsequently, the Commonwealth of Virginia enacted modern legislation, similar to that of the Michigan Comprehensive Reform law. In this legislation, the victim cannot be cross-examined regarding her past sexual history. A victim who alleges that she was raped may still have her reputation within the community come to issue, but testimony about specific sexual acts is expressly prohibited. The victim does not have to prove that she physically resisted the assault. Furthermore, sentencing of the assailant is more flexible with graded penalties, based on the violence of the crime. In May 1979, Shirley Talbert gave a keynote address before the University Association for Emergency Medicine in Orlando, Florida, outlining her organized effort to improve emergency department care of the sexual assault victim. Her speech was especially notable in that she was the only licensed practical nurse to ever address this emergency physician academic organization. In addition, she was the recipient of a community service award from the Charlottesville Board of Supervisors.

As I reflect on this experience, I am certainly pleased that we have improved the quality of care of sexual assault victims. However, I am saddened that I was not aware of the mistreatment of women in our ER until Shirley awakened me from this anaesthetized state. During the last 15 years, I have grown to realize that the problems facing women in our ER in Charlottesville are only the small tip of a giant iceberg that is blocking women from equal status in our country.

These early *life-defining experiences* in our emergency room helped me define my goal: *develop a model emergency medical system for the University of Virginia Hospital as well as the Commonwealth of Virginia*. Faced with numerous life-threatening crises in emergency medical care, I began to search within the massive University medical bureaucracy for other angels to help me. I am delighted to tell you that my search was successful as I found three more unsung heroes at the University who assisted me in dramatically changing emergency care from a fatalistic, disorganized service to a vibrant, structured emergency healthcare system. One was Dr. Ernst Attinger, who was the Director of Biomedical Engineering. Ernst was both a physician and engineer; he was a skilled clinician whose talents in biomedical engineering complemented his innate sensitivity to clinical care.[2] His department had already established contractual relationships with the hospital in which his staff would provide quality assurance testing for medical devices used in the hospital. In addition, he had already established a computerized information system that could be potentially used in the ER.

Another unsung hero was Dr. Richard Crampton, Professor of Cardiology, who had clear visions of the potential benefits of prehospital care in saving the lives of patients with heart attacks. He had developed an effective alliance with one rescue squad, the Charlottesville-Albemarle Rescue Squad, which was willing to develop a prehospital lifesaving plan for patients with heart attacks. Dick first designed this prehospital system so that the rescue squad would pick up a medical resident and transport the resident to the patient with signs of a heart attack. His embryonic program was beginning to save patients' lives. He doggedly pursued his interests in prehospital cardiac care during the subsequent 20 years. He became a recognized leader in this field.

Dr. William H. Muller, Jr., was the third individual who provided invaluable assistance in developing a modern emergency medical system. He was a gifted leader and visionary at our University who carefully guided the growth of the Department of Surgery to national recognition for its excellence in teaching clinical care and research. He developed a management style that differed considerably from heads of surgery in other medical centers. Most department heads purposely restricted the growth of the surgical specialties so that the department would prosper from their clinical income. This jealous guarding of the departmental boundaries markedly restricted the growth of the surgical specialties. Dr. Muller made a dramatic step in managing his department by allowing the specialties in surgery to achieve the same departmental status as his. With the development of the Department of Otolaryngology and Head and Neck Surgery, Department of Neurosurgery, Department of Ophthalmology, Department of Orthopedics, and Department of Plastic Surgery, the Medical School was now able to recruit internationally recognized surgical specialists who were prepared to create world-renowned specialty treatment centers.

Such generosity to the surgical specialty community could have only been expressed by an individual with confidence in himself and his colleagues. Dr. Muller was a world-renowned cardiothoracic surgeon who created an environment in which all individuals could achieve their academic dreams. He predicted that my scientific endeavors might at times be confusing to doubting Thomases. On many occasions, Dr. Muller came to my rescue from the harsh criticisms of eloquent colleagues who feared and resisted change. The fact that I still am a faculty member at the University is a testimony to his successful stewardship and guidance in times of professional battle.

During my tenure as Acting Director of Emergency Medical Services, major developments resulted in dramatic improvements in emergency medical care. Cognizant of the need for improved emergency services in our country, the Robert Wood Johnson Foundation decided in the early 1970s to authorize a nationwide competitive program to encourage communities to develop regional emergency medical systems. In 1974, Dr. Attinger and I were awarded a grant to implement an emergency medical system in our Thomas Jefferson Planning District 10, the five-county geographic catchement area for the University of Virginia Hospital. The grant program, which ended in 1977, focused on access of the public to the emergency medical system by the 911 telephone number, training of rescue squads, and development of a radio communications system for rescue squads in this five-county region. The number 911, designated for public use throughout the United States to request aid from fire, police, or rescue agencies, had already been installed in Nelson County in 1969 after Hurricane Camille.[3] By late 1976, adjacent Greene and Fluvanna Counties had this emergency telephone service. Installation of this system for the more populated regions of Albemarle county and the City of Charlottesville was accomplished in 1984. The development of this 911 telephone system eliminated the 40 telephone numbers for the different police and fire departments and rescue squads in the five-county area. Consequently, we had developed a system that allowed immediate access for hearing individuals into our emergency medical system.

The Department of Transportation's National Highway Safety Administration allocated sufficient funds to develop a training course for rescue personnel that prepared them to care for the sick and injured using basic life-support techniques. This 81-hour training program was pilot-tested at Piedmont Virginia Community College in Charlottesville in 1975, after which it was offered to other rescue squads in the region. Successful completion of the course allowed the rescue squad personnel to be certified as emergency medical technicians-ambulance (EMT-A). In 1983, this training program became the minimum training requirement for the rescue squad personnel for certification by the Virginia Department of Health. The first training program at Piedmont was an Edlich family event. I taught and attended all of the classes and completed certification as an EMT-A. During our mock field tests, my three children, Elizabeth, Richard, and Rachel, volunteered to participate as "casualties."

A radio communications system was designed and implemented by Frank Hunter, Assistant Professor of Biomedical Engineering, that allowed trained rescue squads to communicate with the University of Virginia Medical Center and Martha Jefferson Hospital, as well as with each other. Today, there are three advanced training programs for rescue squads certified by the Virginia Department of Health. The objectives of the emergency medical technician-shock trauma (EMT-ST) training program devised by Diana Rockwell, an emergency medical nurse at our hospital, were to have the student understand the dangerous consequences of significant traumatic injuries and selected medical emergencies, as well as to teach the appropriate therapeutic intervention to stabilize the patient's condition.[4] The emergency medical technician-cardiac (EMT-C) course focused on emergency care of the heart attack patient and taught the student to perform cardiac monitoring and defibrillation, the use of electric shock to correct irregular heartbeats. The emergency medical technician-paramedic course provided the highest level of training for prehospital personnel.

The passage of the Emergency Medical Service Systems Act (EMSS) in 1973 was the next major development. This program, led by David Boyd, authorized $185 million over 10 years and provided the awarding of grants and contracts for development of emergency medical systems throughout the United States. The passage of this Act provided the mechanism and funds for communities in Virginia to develop regional emergency care systems that were modeled after our successful regional system in Charlottesville. Because our system was receiving national recognition, Dr. Boyd asked me to serve as one of his eight physician-technical advisors to assist state governments in designing and implementing their own emergency medical systems. My appointment made me one of Dave's *disciples*, committed to convert state healthcare into an organized emergency medical system. Because Dr. Boyd had developed a clear, conceptual plan for an emergency medical system, our job was relatively easy to advise enthusiastic communities on implementing plans to improve emergency medical care. Because we believed that we were on a medical evangelical mission, his physician/technical advisors served as *disciples,* converting uninformed healthcare workers into an emergency medical team that saved patients' lives.

The only challenging part of my voluntary position was to advise Dr. Cowley regarding his exemplary statewide system that was a model for the world. Realizing that Dr. Cowley was the father of organized trauma care, I willingly accepted the role of student and listened carefully to his retelling of his extensive experience at the Shocktrauma Center. As I carefully reviewed his organized trauma program, I realized that the Commonwealth of Virginia could benefit by replicating his coordinated program.

Dr. Cowley and I spent long hours discussing the many obstacles to implementing a modern trauma care system. In Virginia, I had encountered the same resistance by administrators and surgeons to developing an organized trauma care program that he had overcome in Maryland. On the basis of the pivotal support of Governor Mandel for his trauma care program, he suggested a simple remedy to my problem: enlist the help of the Governor of Virginia. It was fortuitous that the First Lady, Eddy Dalton, and Governor John Dalton were both sympathetic and appreciated the benefits of organized care. When the First Lady joined me on a tour of the Shocktrauma Center in Baltimore, Dr. Cowley provided a clear vision of the components of a successful trauma care system. After an impassioned discussion with Governor Dalton, he directed Virginia's Department of Health to designate regional trauma centers in 1981.

Hospitals designated as trauma centers had to make the commitment detailed in the American College of Surgeons trauma center criteria to develop a responsive program that provides specialized care to the trauma patient.[5] Its designation as a trauma center had considerable influence on the University of Virginia Hospital. There was a positive change in attitude toward the trauma patient by the entire hospital staff, especially surgical and emergency personnel, but also including hospital administrators, teachers, scientists, and support personnel, and gave impetus to the in-house reorganization necessary to develop a highly skilled multidisciplinary trauma service. Today, this service is headed by a nationally recognized leader in trauma care, Dr. Jeff Young, who has trained a skilled staff to care for the trauma patient.

This federally supported program championed by Dr. David Boyd allowed us to implement other important programs in emergency medical care. An emergency first aid guide was written and published in our community telephone books so that each household with a telephone would have an understanding of first aid treatments for the sick and injured. An emergency medical nurse practitioner program was established in the Nursing School that became a fertile training ground for nurses who would assume leadership positions in medicine. One of its graduates, Rebecca Remel, is now the Executive Director of the Pew Charitable Trust in Philadelphia. Linda Richter, after completing her training as a nurse practitioner, established a successful fund-raising program for our School of Nursing. In addition, staff were trained to provide a coordinated, organized approach to the care of the victims of sexual assault, their treatment now guided by modern, updated practices of care. In addition, psychosocial support is arranged for each patient. A computerized poison information system was developed at the UVA hospital that replaced the antiquated card file. Trained staff members now answer each call and ensure optimal care. Trained psychiatrists and social workers staff our crisis intervention center and provide immediate and continued support for all patients. The Hospital employs two full-time nurses to provide continuing education courses for the 18 rescue squads that transport patients to our hospitals. A life support training center was established to teach the faculty and residents the psychomotor skills to care for trauma patients as well as those who have had a heart attack. These trauma and cardiac care programs are accredited educational programs that were instituted in our medical center. Recently, these programs were expanded to include continuing education programs involving the care of the injured or sick child. The cardiac training program has been made available to our fourth-year medical students.

With the exception of an emergency air transportation system, I naively thought that all central Virginia now had immediate access to the finest medical care. This momentary naïve celebration of our accomplishments was shattered when I received a handwritten note from a disgruntled patient. This note became another *life-defining experience*. It opened with a cry for help: "To whom it may concern: I had a frightening experience that I want to share with you. While I was cleaning dishes in the kitchen, I was shocked to see my five-year-old daughter swallow the last portion of a six-ounce bottle of cough syrup. I immediately grabbed the bottle from her hands, thinking that she had swallowed an overdose of medications that may be life-threatening. Using my teletypewriter, I telephoned your poison control center and got no response. Fearing for my daughter's life, I asked my next door neighbor to drive us to the Emergency Room at UVA (the University of Virginia Hospital). Your doctors and nurses were wonderful and assured me that my daughter was in no danger and that the cough syrup would have no side effects. They even showed me some childproof caps for bottles that even I had a hard time opening! The presence of an interpreter who was skilled in sign language considerably facilitated my communication. However, I was shocked to learn that you do not have a TTY (teletypewriter) in your emergency room or hospital. While you have wonderful emergency care for the hearing in your hospital, you have forgotten the deaf." This short letter burst my bubble as I realized that our modern emergency medical system was not responsive to the deaf community. I wrote her an apologetic note, promising that we would have TTYs in the ER as well as the hospital. As per usual, I naively made this promise without speaking to the hospital administrators. Because I purposefully tried to remain uninformed about hospital finances, it was easy for me to make promises without regard to budgets. Through grants from the federal government and the Robert Wood Johnson Foundation, as well as the annual state funding for our hospital, more than $4 million had been spent to develop our modern emergency medical system. Consequently, I thought that the $350.00 needed to buy a TTY would be a drop in this large financial bucket.

I had to develop a written proposal for hospital administration to support the cost of purchasing the TTY for the ER as well as those for the hospital. I wrote the report with the same naïveté of a college student who was submitting a manuscript to his teacher. Because I had not met or treated individuals with severe hearing impairments, I had no perception of the plight of the deaf community. To familiarize hospital administrators with the importance of the project, I went immediately to our library to search for information on the TTY system that could be included in my report. This report began by describing the origin of the TTY so that the administrators would be better able to understand its purpose. It went something like this: "A major development in telecommunications enabled deaf individuals to use standard telephone technology to transmit messages between teletypewriters. In 1964, Robert

Wietbrecht, a deaf physicist, developed a modem (MODulator-DE-Modulator) to convert teletypewriter code into frequency or tones that are transmitted over telephone lines. When receiving, the demodulator circuits of the modem convert the tones into the digital signals used by a teleprinter. More than 75,000 deaf people have the special teletypewriters/ telecommunications devices (TTY/TDD) that allow them to send and receive messages by telephone and gain access to emergency care. This telecommunications device must be immediately purchased and available for use in the ER and poison control center. In addition, a TTY should be available for patients with hearing impairment to be used in their hospital rooms. The retail cost for this device is $350.00."

My proposal was sent expeditiously to hospital administration with the expectation that I would receive an A for its content and $700.00 for TTYs in the ER and poison control center. One week later, the hospital administrator gave me an F and no check, explaining that the funding for my request would be placed in next year's proposed hospital budget. While the eloquent letter from the deaf mother had touched my heart, my scholarly manuscript on TTYs had not opened the hospital coffers. Dismayed by the failure of the hospital to implement this lifesaving system for the deaf, I telephoned the hospital administrator and reiterated the importance of TTYs to our hospital and even threw in the medical and legal implications of our failure to have TTYs. My pleas fell on deaf ears. . .

My disappointment with the hospital's lack of support for the deaf community, coupled with the weight of my promise to the distressed mother that our hospital would serve the deaf community, propelled me to search for another avenue to solve our problem, one that would also help deaf individuals throughout the state of Virginia: the development of a statewide emergency telecommunication system for the deaf. I sent in a grant request to the Office of Emergency Services located in the state government of the Commonwealth of Virginia. I provided a detailed description of the system that could be available at a bargain price of $25,000.00. A computer-aided emergency telecommunication system for the deaf would be housed in our poison control center and serve as a relay station for all TTY calls from the deaf. My grant for an innovative emergency program for the deaf community throughout the state was turned down by the Office of Emergency Services with the explanation that such a statewide program would be better coordinated by its Richmond office. It is important, however, to point out that my rejection letter did not include any promise by the office that such a program would be implemented.

Undeterred by this bad news, I then pursued yet another avenue for solving this urgent problem: garnering funds for the development of a nationwide emergency telecommunications system for the deaf. With the appropriate modifications, I expanded my proposal, describing a computer-aided emergency telecommunications system for the deaf for the entire country at a bargain price of only $250,000. I sent this grant request into the Office of Emergency Services of the Department of Health and Human Services of the federal government. I did not have any unrealistic expectations of successful grant approval because this division had planned to be terminated; moreover, my benefactor and friend, David Boyd, had resigned from the office. Consequently, my next letter of rejection from the federal government came as no surprise. Despite this growing list of rejections for my plans for an emergency telecommunications system for the deaf, I remained blissfully optimistic that I would achieve my new *goal* of developing a nationwide system and keep my promise to the deaf mother. I realized that the reasons for my unsuccessful attempts to assist the deaf community were caused primarily by the fact that I was communicating with decision-makers who were unsympathetic to the plight of the deaf community. I had to find an individual or organization who listened to the deaf.

I found the answer to my search in a hotel room in Chicago.[6] The reason for my visit to Chicago was the annual meeting of the American College of Surgeons. Because my academic career had required increasing numbers of trips, I felt considerable loneliness, missing my wife and three children living on our 18-acre farm in Albemarle County, twelve miles from the University. On Sunday mornings, I decided to try to find some spiritual consolation watching a televised church service. During this telecast, I must confess that I did not recognize the name of the minister, but I was impressed by his strong voice, commitment to beautiful music and God. What mostly caught my attention was a small box in the lower right-hand corner of the screen in which a woman was using sign language to communicate the minister's message to the deaf while the sermon was being delivered. Because I had presumed that this televised service originated in Illinois, I did not believe that this minister was the individual who could answer my prayers for a partner in my planned nationwide communication system for the deaf. The distance between Chicago and the University of Virginia would make such a partnership, at best, difficult to achieve. The credits at the end of the telecast provided the answer to my quest when they identified the service as being broadcast from the Thomas Road Baptist Church in Lynchburg, Virginia.

When I returned home to Charlottesville, I called the church to learn the name of this televangelist. The operator at the church informed me that Reverend Jerry Falwell was the minister whose Sunday services were televised throughout the world as the "Old Time Gospel Hour." Believing that my position at the University of Virginia would allow me easy access to Reverend Falwell, I was surprised to learn from his appointment secretary that his schedule was so filled for the next six months that he would not be able to meet with me.

Humbled by this news, I realized that I would have to get a friend in Lynchburg to bypass the appointment secretary. It was fortuitous that I had developed a close friendship with Dr. Stuart Harris who is one of the most respected surgeons in Virginia. Stuart is a Lynchburg legend who is known throughout the state. After being a football star in high school in Lynchburg, he became a student athlete at the University of Virginia. While excelling in football, he achieved an excellent academic record that allowed him admission to the University of Virginia School of Medicine. After completing his surgical training, he returned to Lynchburg to be its premier general surgeon. Stuart and I had completed several clinical studies that were published in peer-reviewed surgical journals. I made a telephone call to Stuart, asking that he arrange a meeting on my behalf with Dr. Falwell. Without asking me the reason for my visit, he assured me that he would arrange it. Before my visit with Dr. Falwell, I collected some information about him that would prepare me for the meeting. I had hoped that this review would allow me to ascertain whether he was a visionary who could realize big dreams. Here is what I found.

On June 21, 1956, 35 adults and children met with Jerry Falwell in the Mountain View Elementary School in Lynchburg for the first worship service of a new church. Since that time, the Thomas Road Baptist Church has grown to include a congregation of 22,000 members, a Christian academy, a Bible institute, a seminary, and a four-year university. Each week, six million viewers watch the Sunday morning service on television, and millions more hear Dr. Falwell by radio. Reverend Falwell attributes his remarkable growth to his faith in God and has said, "I believe God and mountains have been moved." Realizing that if he could move mountains, he could easily be my partner in developing a National Crisis Center for the Deaf.

Fully aware of the importance of this meeting, I brought with me respected colleagues from the University who could eloquently vouch for the importance of the mission. Dr. Will Spradlin, Professor and Chairman of the Department of Psychiatry, and Dr. Daniel Spyker, Director of the new computerized Poison Control Center, agreed to join me for the mission. We met Reverend Falwell in his office at the Thomas Road Baptist Church. After introducing my colleagues to him, I outlined our plans for a computerized emergency telecommunications system for the deaf in the United States. When I began to discuss the need for such a program, he asked me politely to expedite my discussion because he reminded me that he had long been a champion for the deaf and had been committed to their access to his ministry using signing as well as TTYs. I then indicated that this communication center would be housed at both his University and at the University of Virginia. Staff from his university could provide spiritual counsel to the deaf, while the University of Virginia would coordinate emergency services. I handed him a proposal for the telecommunication centers. Without reading it, he asked the big question: "How much money will you need?" I answered, "$250,000.00." He immediately responded, "I can support your proposal. Let's get started as soon as possible."

In June 1981, two years after I read the deaf mother's impassioned plea, the National Emergency Medical Telecommunications System for the Deaf was established. The deaf community had 24-hour, toll-free access to this center which is staffed by emergency personnel especially trained to meet the communication needs of the deaf. Our computerized system expedited exchange by automatically sending out questions. The staff member monitors this interchange between the deaf caller and the microcomputer and interrupts as needed to elicit additional information or clarify responses. A computerized directory of emergency services facilitates referral to an appropriate public agency. After identifying the agency, the staff member telephones the agency, requesting a response to the caller's emergency situation. Within the first month, our staff responded to calls from 20 states as well as the District of Columbia.

We were very surprised by the different types of calls. Sixty-one percent of the callers used the emergency service for information referral. Because deaf individuals had no access to banks, utility companies, or directory assistance, they viewed themselves as isolated from society and in desperate need of assistance in conducting the business of their everyday lives. While hearing individuals telephone a bank about checks, loans, and mortgages, banks, like hospitals, have no TTY to receive calls from the deaf community. Consequently, the deaf community appropriately judges calls to a utility company or bank to be an emergency. Only 24% of the callers requested lifesaving emergency care. The remaining callers (15%) requested that our staff relay information to members of the hearing community. The type of information relayed included contact with employers to give notice of illness, personal business inquiries, and notification of death of a family member. Our joint effort clearly demonstrated that the deaf community throughout the country was isolated from society and subject to discrimination because of their disability. This unconscionable and deplorable situation was finally resolved with the passage of the American with Disabilities Act (ADA) in 1990. Because this Act required that each local telephone system design an emergency response system for the deaf, the need for our pilot program ended.

Our attempts to improve communication and safety for the deaf community facilitated the vast changes implemented by the ADA. In watching this revolution take place, I learned a very important lesson. The pursuit of a dream that changes lives is so grand it cannot be contained. Its power radiates, takes on a life of its own, and provides the blueprint for other changes and contributions in areas that were never identified from the outset. This ripple effect demonstrates the power of perseverance. It also shows that gifts will arise out of the process itself. I learned that solutions and answers are many times found in embracing the support and vision of unsung heroes, and in watching for opportunities wherever I am or in whatever I am doing. The answer lies in unleashing the power we all have within us.

Because I was part of Dr. David Boyd's revolutionary medical adventure, I thought it should be documented in the scientific literature. Dave expressed some reluctance in collaborating in this endeavor because he was too busy changing our nation's healthcare system. Fortunately, in 1983, he agreed to edit with me and Dr. Sylvia Micik, Associate Professor of Clinical Pediatrics at the University of California School of Medicine in San Diego, the landmark publication, *Systems Approach to Emergency Medical Care*.[7] In our preface to this book, we pointed out, "This book is of importance to EMS systems today as few, if any, regional EMS systems have yet to accomplish the task of completing a totally comprehensive regional EMS system." This prediction was verified by a report in the Journal of the American Medical Association in 1989 that acknowledged that only Virginia and Maryland had successfully implemented all components of a comprehensive regional EMS system. Today, our hospital has a new emergency department with modern critical care facilities. The emergency department is directed and staffed by physicians trained in emergency medicine. A residency training program has been established to train future leaders in academic emergency medicine.

A recent development in emergency medical services has been the establishment of an emergency air transportation system. The emergency air transportation system began on a beautiful fall day in 1975 when we were contacted by a physician in Grundy, Virginia, requesting that we accept a burn patient in transfer to our hospital. Because the ground transportation distance from Grundy to Charlottesville is more than 9 hours, I knew that this seriously ill burn patient would die of shock during the long ambulance ride. Knowing that I could possibly save the patient's life if I had a plane to fly there and back, I rented a fixed-wing aircraft to fly me to Grundy. After gathering together appropriate lifesaving equipment, I began our first emergency medical flight for the University Hospital. I must confess that it was a spectacular adventure flying over the beautiful mountains of Virginia on such a magnificent day.

When I arrived in Grundy, I was met by an ambulance that transported me to the hospital. After stabilizing the condition of this desperately ill young man, we transported him back to the airport. The patient was accompanied by his father, who wanted to join us. I welcomed him to fly with us, but I was concerned that he would have no place to stay in Charlottesville. He assured me that he would be very comfortable sleeping in the lobby of the University Hospital. When a nurse in Grundy asked if he had enough money for food, he indicated that he did not have enough if his son's hospitalization lasted longer than a week. Without hesitation, she opened her purse and gave him $40 to help him on his journey. This generous gift from the nurse exemplifies the gifts of love and affection that I have encountered from so many loving individuals during my travels through emergency medicine during the last 20 years. We transported the patient back to the hospital where he made an uneventful recovery. When I presented the bill for renting the plane to the Director of the hospital, he looked at me with considerable surprise and asked if I planned to continue these rescue operations. I assured him that this first flight was just the beginning. My prediction has become a reality with the development of the Pegasus Flight Operations.

Prescription for Healing

For each patient, a system of care must be devised that provides treatment from the time of illness or injury until complete recovery.

Most health professionals and patients view patient care as episodic events in which symptoms and signs of a disease are being treated and become the focus of attention. Because of the health professional's training as well as time constraints, the psychosocial complexity of the whole patient may not be understood.

An efficient healthcare system involves a multidisciplinary team of skilled individuals whose role in healthcare must be carefully coordinated. The ultimate patient outcome is dependent on all members of this team.

With the exception of emergency medical systems, healthcare has rarely been conceived of as a system of care in which all members of the team are valued. In a recent survey of the attitudes of physicians, they graded their societal value to be more than any other group, with the exception of God. With such high personal regard, one can now understand why physicians find it difficult to be team players.

The efficacy of all aspects of a healthcare system must be carefully monitored using measurable outcomes that can be accurately determined.

In an emergency medical system, response times to the scene of the accident and transport to the hospital are pivotal determinants of performance. If the response is delayed, the system is corrected immediately. Such outcome measures are not rigorously used in other patient management. Because outcome measures are rarely recorded in the management of each individual patient, it is difficult for the healthcare system to take corrective action.

All members of the healthcare team must participate in specific job training courses that allow them to be certified by an agency.

Because job requirements involve learning specific psychomotor skills, simulated training programs must be designed to evaluate performance. The educational system of health professionals is based on an outdated paradigm that assumes the health professional can assimilate any and all information and that it will remain valid. Because healthcare information can no longer be understood by any individual, teachers desperately try to teach excessive amounts of information that the student cannot possibly absorb. Overpowered by the amount of cognitive information that the student must learn, psychomotor skill training is largely ignored. Most physicians are ill-prepared to care for seriously ill patients.

Health professionals must practice and master psychomotor skills on simulators rather than on human beings.

Psychomotor skill training for physicians should be accomplished in a manner similar to professional pilots learning to fly airplanes. Pilots repeatedly use developed flight simulation models that allow them to practice using the instruments without flying the plane. The medical profession has been more reluctant to use simulation models for education. Dr. Wangensteen would be the first to acknowledge the importance of residents practicing canine surgery before mastering surgery in humans. When applicable, he favored learning experiences using mechanical simulators, avoiding surgery on animals. Being reared on the farm, he had developed a great love and affection for animals that assured appropriate and kind management of animals in his experimental research laboratory.

The healthcare worker must nurture and support the soul of the injured or ill patient.

The pain of the patient is perceived in many different ways by family and friends. All members of the healthcare team must have sufficient psychosocial training that allows them to be *present* with the patient *in the moment* and to implement follow-up plans that remind the patient that the hospital team is always prepared to lend an assisting hand.

The conceptual design of the system must be continually updated to meet the ever-changing needs of society.

While systems are learning new information about natural environmental disasters, the causes of mass casualties are constantly changing with the advent of international terrorism. The system must gain new information and new techniques to handle dramatic changes in society.

During its 10 years of operation, Pegasus has transported 5,945 patients by helicopter and 1,393 patients by fixed wing. In 1998, 571 critically ill patients were transferred by helicopter to the University of Virginia Hospital. The majority of the patients (68%) flown by helicopter were transferred from a referring hospital to us. The remaining patients (32%) were stabilized by the trained rescue squad at the scene of the accident and then transferred to the Emergency Department of the University of Virginia Hospital.

The fixed-wing air transport team made 205 flights. Of these, 135 flights involved the transfer of critically ill patients. In 70 other flights, our transplant team procured organ donations. Our newborn ICU accounts for approximately 5% of the fixed-wing flights, as well as helicopter flights bringing critically ill babies back to the University's neonatal ICU.

I have tried to show, dramatically and graphically, how patients with life-threatening illnesses or injuries, who once would have died during transport to the nearest emergency department are now being safely transported to our exemplary University Hospital that is prepared to take heroic measures to save the patients' lives. Most of these survivors are rescued by a well-trained team of health professionals who gain little national recognition. However, when Christopher Reeve suffered a spinal chord injury after falling from his horse in nearby Culpeper, Virginia, every American celebrated his emergency medical and rehabilitation journey. It was indeed fortunate that his injury occurred after the implementation of this modern emergency medical system. I fear that the treatment of this same injury in the 1970s could have been the toe tag and a courteous dispatch to the morgue.

As doctors, nurses, paramedics, pilots, and rescue squad volunteers save lives, they are faced with tremendous emotional pressures in their efforts to reverse the tide of violent death. Breathtaking in its immediacy, moving in its intimacy, and exhilarating in its message of hope, it has been an unforgettable saga of an emergency medical adventure that we are still waging together. As I reflect on my career in emergency medicine over the last 20 years, I have had the unrivaled honor of championing the development of a model emergency medical system in Virginia that has saved thousands of lives. The success of this emergency medical system is because of the talented members of the emergency medical team who care for the patient from the time of injury until complete recovery. My professional career has truly been a joyful experience. I have ridden the winged horse Pegasus to a constellation in the stars. I am one of the luckiest people in the world to have been privileged to be a part of this heavenly adventure.

Other gifted physicians, like Dr. Ronald Krome, have commented on the honor of being one of the pioneers in the genesis of emergency medical care. He, like myself, feels genuinely blessed to have followed in the footsteps of Mills, Cowley, and Boyd, and has witnessed the realization of their vision. He provided a unique perception of the extraordinary people involved in this medical adventure as well as its importance: "Most of us were not Nobel Laureates in medicine; we never discovered a cure for cancer or an immunization or cure for AIDS. But I think that we changed the face of American medicine for all time. There are very few people in the history of healthcare and medicine who have had the opportunity to do that and ever did that. Our generation did."

Realizing the importance of the development of emergency medical care, I have outlined the *profiles for success* for healing in prescriptions that should be helpful to all healthcare workers, regardless of their *goals*. The lay persons would also benefit from this information so that they can demand excellent healthcare in their communities.

6

Patient's Voyage

"Medicine in the United States is widely recognized as the best in the world. Hardly a day passes without a major scientific breakthrough. Many formerly fatal diseases are now curable. People are healthier and live longer than ever. Still, patient dissatisfaction with doctors has rarely been more acute. Although physicians are increasingly able to cure disease and prolong life, the American public is suspicious, distrustful of, even antagonistic to, the profession. Doctors, uneasy, astonished, resentful and angry, universally acknowledge a crisis in healthcare."

Bernard Lown, MD

The pressures on clinicians who are treating *patients*, particularly children, with presently incurable diseases are clearly shown in the acclaimed film, *Lorenzo's Oil*.[1] There is a sense of medical and personal desperation when a child has a disease that is likely to be progressive and fatal that empowers families and doctors to search for treatments that may save the child's life. It might be helpful to begin this discussion by reflecting on this movie.

A young American boy, Lorenzo, is playing on the beach in Comoro Islands off of the east African coast. He is being taught to fly a kite by his adolescent companion, a native of the island, Amouri. As they watch the kite in the blue sky, Amouri recites to Lorenzo the words from a Swahili warrior song: "Life has meaning only in the struggle. Triumph or defeat is in the hands of the gods. So let us celebrate the struggle." Lorenzo subsequently departs from this picturesque island with his father, Augusto Odone, and his mother, Michaela, to return to the United States. An officer of the World Bank, Augusto is returning to his home office located in Washington, D.C. During the next year, they note that their beloved son develops considerable difficulty walking; his disability is the beginning of a *life-defining experi-*

ence. Because Lorenzo is their beloved son, his illness causes them to be *present in the moment.*

Michaela and Augusto consult with a physician at Washington Children's Hospital to learn the following information: "There is a family of diseases that is quite rare: the leukodystrophies. Lorenzo has one of them. It is called ALD, adrenoleukodystrophy. ALD is an inborn error of metabolism that causes a degeneration of the brain. It only affects males, usually between the ages of 5 and 10. Its progress is relentless, the end is inevitable. All boys with ALD die, usually within two years of diagnosis." The distraught Michaela responds, "And there are no exceptions?" The doctor laments, "I am so sorry. . ."

Michaela questions again: "Are you absolutely sure?" The doctor provides a convincing argument for his diagnosis: "Yes, Lorenzo shows the definitive sign. He has an abnormally high level of fat in his blood, certain very long chains of saturated fats . . . there is an enzyme that should metabolize these fats, but in ALD boys, it is defective, so they collect in nerve cells, a little like cholesterol in the arteries, and in some way, this liquefies the white matter of the brain. . . Myelin is the fatty sheath that insulates the nerves, a little like plastic around electric wires. Without it, the nerves cannot conduct an impulse. What ALD does is strip away the myelin; it corrodes it, if you like. This causes degeneration of the brain and, as the brain degenerates, the body loses its functions." Michaela, searching for hope, responds: "Then there is absolutely no treatment?" Shaking his head, the doctor says, "No."

Later, the determined Augusto visits a medical library, reading articles on this fatal inherited disease. After reviewing one of the articles, he retreats to a stairwell, falls down and cries hysterically. Realizing that his screams for help were falling on deaf ears, he defined his new *goal: cure our son's illness.*

Augusto's search continues for additional advice from powerful *problem-solvers.* He is referred to Dr. Gus Nicholias, Professor of Neurology at the Institute in Childhood Diseases in Washington, D.C., who is considered to be the world's expert on leukodystrophies, working on an experimental protocol using a new diet. During the meeting with Dr. Nicholias, he explains to Michaela and Augusto more about the causal factors of ALD. "The human body needs these fats (saturated fats) in order to create cells. The excess is burned off. That's normal, of course, but in the case of an ALD boy, these saturates can't be broken down and they build up in the brain." He later indicates that, if he could successfully withdraw the saturated fat from the diet, he would prevent them from accumulating in the brain. He points out that there is no way to reverse the neurological disease: "All we can hope for is to slow down the cascade of symptoms."

Dr. Nicholias asked Lorenzo to participate in the trials of his new diet that was designed to suppress the build-up of the dangerous saturated very long chain fatty acids (VLCFA). As the conversation continues, Dr. Nicholias informs Augusto and Michaela that ALD is passed only through the mother: ". . . ALD is only carried on the female chromosome." The despondent and incredulous mother exclaims, "Excuse me? Are you saying that Lorenzo got this directly from me?" Dr. Nicholias confirms that the ALD gene is sex-linked and that it goes from mother to son. He further explains that the woman is only a carrier and has a 50/50 chance of passing on the defect to her male children. He makes the callous comment, "That it is the cruelest kind of genetic lottery. . ." Michaela's sister later explains her feelings about this "genetic lottery." "She feels incredibly alone and incredibly unlucky, like she has been singled out by God."

Their journey for a cure continues as Michaela and Augusto take their son to Boston for further consultation. Lorenzo's case is presented to a conference in an amphitheater packed full of doctors where Lorenzo is asked to walk painfully across the stage. This medical conference graphically depicts the insensitivity and callousness of the medical process, where the terrified child is left to ask in his quavering voice, "Why are all these people here?" The physician in charge of the conference impolitely uses medical terminology that is understandable only to his colleagues and makes no effort to communicate with the child or his family. It was a freak show in which the healers appear as artists involved only in drawing an accurate picture of the disease, rather than curing it.

With Lorenzo now being in a pilot study using a new diet, Michaela and Augusto seek advice and support from an ALD charity that sponsors ALD support groups. At the first meeting they attend, they are surprised to find parents of other children with ALD who are also in the pilot study. During the meeting, parents begin to step forward in large numbers and sadly admit that their children have not benefited from Dr. Nicholias' diet as measured by the levels of saturated fatty acids in the blood. The charity's president desperately tries to control the mood of the dissatisfied group. He hastily explains that, "The pilot study on the diet has to run the full six months. We're not scientists. We don't take it on ourselves to interpret experiments. That's the responsibility of the doctors." A mother responds to the charity president's comments by saying, "So what you are saying is that our children are in the service of medical science? How very foolish of me. . ..! I always assumed that medical science was in the service of the sufferers!" In our modern healthcare system, this mother's comment seemed to resonate society's discontent with the medical profession.

Realizing that Lorenzo has no effective advocates in the medical profession or supporting charities, the Odones, without medical credentials, begin their courageous journey to cure their son's illness. In speaking to his wife, Augusto comments, "In order to understand ALD, we need a command of genetics, biochemistry, microbiology, neurology, etc.. . ." Overwhelmed by this ambitious proposal, she counters, "We don't have time to go to medical school!" Augusto goes directly to the heart of the problem, "The doctors are groping in the dark. They've got Lorenzo on a topsy-turvy diet, bloody immunosuppressants . . . it is brutal and useless. We should not consign it blindly into their hands. He should not suffer by our ignorance. We take responsibility. We read a little, and go out and inform ourselves." While he searches through the literature, Augusto also organizes a symposium of the leading scientific *powerful problem-solvers* studying ALD, hoping to reach a consensus and devise a plan to cure his son's illness. He served as a moderator for this forum to ensure that the distinguished scientists accomplished their objective. The Odones are committed to transforming a *crisis into an opportunity*.

The Odones' journey is well-defined and unique. They empowered themselves to be partners in a search for a cure, rather than be spectators. In my own experience, the patient and family members often give their power over to the treating physician, whom they view as omnipotent. This total relegation of responsibility may be comfortable to some doctors because it prevents an effective dialogue, but it is really a missed opportunity. If the physicians view their patients as partners in care, physicians find their patients will become their teachers. In addition, empowered patients will be carefully informed about their treatments and will comply responsibly to achieve a successful outcome.

The Odones' research led to a *societal transformation* of the treatment of ALD.[2] They used erucic acid (22 carbon monounsaturated fatty acid) for dietary suppression of VLCFA levels. Supplementation of the diet of ALD patients with an oil, now called Lorenzo's oil, in combination with the restriction of dietary intake of saturated VLCFA has been found to lower the levels of plasma-saturated VLCFA to normal levels within a relatively short time. Lorenzo's oil consists of a mixture of two triglycerides: glycerol trioleate and glycerol trierucate, glycerol esters of oleic and erucic acid. In response to the Odones' therapeutic triumph, it comes as no surprise that the ALD Foundation refuses to acknowledge this diet as a cure because it had not been medically validated. Despite the lack of scientific support for their potentially curative treatment, the movie ends with the following comments: "Doctors all over the world have begun to prescribe Lorenzo's oil. If a diagnosis is given early enough, the treatment stops the disease. So now there is a growing army of boys kept free from the ravages of ALD."

In recognition of his efforts, Augusto Odone has received an honorary medical degree. He and Michaela continue to raise funds and direct the scientific taskforce known as the Myelin Project. The goal of this project is to *grow successfully new myelin in the brains of older ALD patients, like Lorenzo, who developed brain injury before this miraculous oil was discovered.*

In 1995, Professor Hugo W. Moser[3] of the Departments of Neurology and Pediatrics of Johns Hopkins Hospital commented about the development of Lorenzo's oil in a published scientific article. "In light of the concern about the safety of oils high in erucic acid and the possibility that patients with ALD might not be able to metabolize this very-long-chain monounsaturated fatty acid, the medical community, ourselves included, was hesitant to consider the use of erucic acid for ALD therapy. However, as depicted so vividly in the motion picture, *Lorenzo's Oil,* the Odone family, whose son is severely disabled by ALD, persuaded the Croda Universal Ltd. Company in England to produce a highly purified oil comprised of a 4:1 mixture of glyceryl trioleate and glyceryl trierucate. This mixture is now referred to as Lorenzo's oil in honor of their son. In collaboration with Dr. William Rizzo and associates (Section on Biochemical Genetics, National Institute of Child Health and Human Development, Bethesda, Maryland), the Odones demonstrated that this oil has a powerful effect on the levels of saturated VLCFA assays in plasma. The oil normalized the plasma level of C26:0 within four weeks and appeared to have few side effects. The dramatic biochemical effect of Lorenzo's oil led us and others to abandon the trials with glyceryl trioleate oil alone and to undertake clinical evaluations of this new substance."

In 1995, Dr. Moser was honored to give the distinguished Komrower Lecture in which he discussed the treatment of ALD. During the last four years, he conducted an open trial of Lorenzo's oil therapy in 53 patients with ALD who were without neurological symptoms at the time that the therapy was initiated. On the basis of his study, he concluded that the results in the 53 patients seem more favorable than those in these historical series, and *suggest that the Lorenzo's oil therapy can reduce the frequency and severity of subsequent neurological involvement in ALD patients who are treated before they have neurological symptoms.* In his study of older children with ALD who had neurological symptoms, he reported that, "Lorenzo's oil therapy does not have a clinically significant effect on quality of life or the progression of this severe illness." The patients continued to become more disabled and several families elected to discontinue the diet since they did not wish to impose its restrictions on a child who had so many other problems and so few sources of pleasure. Dr. Moser concludes that, "Lorenzo's oil therapy alone in patients who are already neurologically symptomatic does not appear to provide clinically significant benefit and may not be justified because of the change in lifestyle imposed on a child who already has so many problems and the risk of side-effects such as reduced platelet count. However, as other modes of therapy evolve, the dietary therapy may serve as an adjunct." He then points out that other therapies for ALD are emerging. These include bone marrow transplantation . . . and gene therapy.

Michaela and Augusto have brought real hope to the asymptomatic child, but they have not solved Lorenzo's severe neurological problems. Lorenzo, now 19, remains in bed and requires 24-hour nursing assistance.

In 1997, I visited Augusto on a Monday at his Myelin Project headquarters office located on Pennsylvania Avenue in Washington, D.C. He was an hour late for my appointment. Dressed casually in a polo shirt and light blue pants, he first politely apologized for his late arrival. He looked very fatigued, attributing it to his and his wife's participation in the care of Lorenzo over the weekend. He pointed out the difficulty in finding nurses to work weekend shifts. He asked if I knew any nurses in Charlottesville who would be willing to work in his home. At that moment, I realized that he was consumed by his son's illness, serving as personal caretaker, nursing assistant and champion for a cure of his son's illness.

He remained optimistic about his son's future, hoping that he would soon find a way to grow new myelin in his son's brain. His foundation supports targeted research programs throughout the world whose *goal* is to remyelinate the brains of children with ALD. Because patients with multiple sclerosis (MS) have evidence of loss of myelin in their brains and spinal cords, he believes that his research will also benefit patients with MS. He points out that a gene for ALD has recently been identified. This finding will provide a major impetus toward the development of better therapeutic strategies for his son. If he is unable to remyelinate Lorenzo's brain, a cure for the devastating condition may have to wait for gene replacement therapy.

I talked with him about his scientific journey to cure his son's illness. He explained to me that the major passion in his life was to cure ALD. He had carefully crafted a scientific journey that could lead to a successful outcome. He had ingeniously enlisted the support of scientists and generous donors to achieve this *goal*. He focused his Myelin Project on patient's with ALD as well as those individuals with MS. Because ALD affects less than 5,000 to 10,000 children, this number is not significant enough to raise the awareness and conscience of our society. Consequently, he has wisely linked his program with MS research. He engagingly hints that his research program could benefit the 400,000 patients with MS. My discussions with him confirmed that he had little understanding of MS, but clearly, he was the world's expert on ALD.

When I watched the movie, *Lorenzo's Oil*, I thought that Augusto had developed some well-deserved distrust for physicians, scientists and charities. He confirmed my suspicions with a smile and did not give my questions any energetic response, realizing that it would interfere with his quest. When physicians care for patients with such illnesses, their most common approach is to refer them to an "expert" in treating the disease. For the expert to be successful in the search of a cure, there must be a focused pursuit of the *goal* similar to that of Augusto and Michaela in their search for a cure for their son's illness. Because the road to a cure is filled with many obstacles, the expert may begin to search for ways to lose that focus, rather than deal with the painful realization that the expert may fail to find a cure. For example, some experts, valiantly searching for the cure for cancer, have ended up "growing" it in their laboratories, becoming the world's authorities on cancer cultivation. They become a connoisseur of cancer growth and begin to view it as a flower or a kiss of death, rather than a brutal devastating killer. Families of patients with incurable diseases and the patient do not have the luxury of losing this focus and must valiantly continue to search for the cure. In the inspirational story of the Odones' search for a cure for their son's illness, it was bewildering to see the experts, in their failed attempts at a cure, become the greatest impediment to the Odone's quest.

There is a growing realization that the patient and family member must take charge of their illness in a partnership with the healthcare workers. The patient and family understand that a cure can only be achieved by this intimate alliance. With advances in information technology, there are now unique opportunities for patients and their families to get advice regarding physicians who specialize in the care of their illness. I am delighted that such a service has been started by an innovative individual who was trying to cure his own illness.

In 1986, Gregory White Smith was diagnosed with an inoperable brain tumor and given only months to live by two doctors at major medical centers. Refusing to believe this bleak prognosis, Smith decided to seek the best doctor available to treat his condition in hopes of curing his tumor. Smith did have a distinct advantage in his search for the best doctor. He and his colleague, Steven Naifeh, both Harvard Law School graduates, had left behind successful law careers to become writers. In 1983, they completed *The Best Lawyers in America*[4], a "guide to the best and brightest in the legal profession." Through extensive telephone interviews asking professionals to rate their peers, they had developed an unrivaled method for evaluating the quality of professional services.

After finding the best doctor for Smith, who is currently alive and in excellent condition, the two men performed the same service for the medical profession as they had for the legal profession. Today, what started as a single biennial publication, *The Best Doctors in America*[5], has grown into the largest medical information services company of its kind in the world, with Smith serving as the vice-president of *Best Doctors*! Each year, a staff of 25 people surveys more than 35,000 physicians and processes more than a million individual evaluations. Because it is based on peer review, *The Best Doctors in America* has been eagerly received by patients as well as the medical community.

Over the last ten years, *Best Doctors* has built the largest and most comprehensive database on doctor quality in the world, including almost every medical specialty and physicians from more than 150 countries around the world. This database allows patients to find the best medical care whenever and wherever they need it. Patients, such as a traveling executive in a foreign country, parents with a sick child in a new hometown, or simply an individual who has been diagnosed with a serious illness and wants a second opinion or treatment from a top specialist, can benefit from this database.

At a time when there is increasing demand for information on the comparative quality of competing medical services, *Best Doctors* has made it its mission to develop that information and make it available to those who need it. Their unique method of assessing the quality of medical professionals has earned extraordinary respect both inside and outside the medical community. Their assessments continue to improve the quality and effectiveness of medical care for individuals around the world. Their public information system empowers the patient and family to take charge of their illness and be a partner with the healthcare worker. The sick and injured can now seize the day!

Physician-as-Patient's Quest

"It is fair to say that the physician is never justified in giving up on any case, or in saying or doing anything that weakens the patient's determination to do his or her own part of the job. Although we ought never to underestimate the seriousness of a medical problem, it is equally important never to underestimate the ability of the patient to mount a prodigious response to the challenge of disease."

Norman Cousins, Ph.D.

On February 11, 1985, I can assure you that I was ill-prepared for this next *life-defining experience*, joining the physician-as-patient community. I had just returned from a medical meeting in Richmond, Virginia, feeling all the signs and symptoms of an impending cold, including runny nose, low-grade fever, and headache. Consequently, I went to bed immediately after my arrival at home, hoping to thwart the encroaching flu-like symptoms. The next morning, I was frightened that those symptoms had transformed into a profound weakness in both my legs, rendering me incapable of walking. Fearing that I had developed an infection in my brain or spinal cord, I asked my wife to call my primary care physician as well as the rescue squad to transfer me to the hospital. Bypassing the emergency department that I had founded, I was escorted immediately to a private room in which my primary care physician and neurologist were prepared to diagnose and treat my condition.

Because my inability to walk was my most life-threatening physical finding, my primary care physician allowed the neurologist to supervise my care. His physical examination confirmed the weakness in both extremities that was associated with a reduced sensitivity to touch. When he tested my reflexes in my knees, I noted that my knee jerks were hyperactive in both legs. His comments were short, but comforting. First, he shared with me that he was not certain of the cause of my illness.

He warned me that he thought that my condition was serious, but not grave enough to ask my children to return to Charlottesville. Tomorrow he promised he would perform additional studies that would provide further insight into my diagnosis. He ordered a magnetic resonance imaging test of my brain and spinal cord, after which he would perform a spinal tap.

The next day started immediately with my transfer to a stretcher that allowed me a new view of the tiling and fluorescent lights lining the ceiling of the hospital hallways. My tour and visit of the magnetic imaging facility was an expeditious one because the staff gave me VIP treatment, placing me ahead of the queue of other patients. Upon returning to my room, the neurologist greeted me with sterile surgical gloves and an open spinal tap tray. After being transferred to my bed, he performed the diagnostic spinal tap with considerable skill. It was comforting to me that he had maintained his skills in a procedure that was done most commonly by residents in a university hospital. He indicated that I should rest peacefully in my bed the rest of the day. He pointed out that an evoked response test would be done tomorrow. This test measures the electric response to stimulation of the eye, recorded through surface electrodes on my scalp. He indicated that the results of these studies would all be available in two days, allowing him to make a diagnosis of my condition.

He set up an appointment to meet with me in my hospital room to review the results of these studies. He said that he was going to place a "no visitors" sign on my door to protect me from that anticipated deluge of colleagues, residents, and students who would be interested in supporting me. I can assure you that this sign was extremely effective in isolating me in my corner of the university hospital. One benefit of this social isolation was that it allowed me to be *present in the moment* with the signs and symptoms of a serious illness. It was fortuitous that my wife was able to break though this isolation barrier and provide me with emotional support. Telephone calls from my three children also were very consoling in my new role as physician–as–patient. My new role as a patient became my next *life-defining experience*.

As promised, the neurologist arrived promptly to give me the results of the diagnostic studies. He began by telling me the good news in that I had no evidence of a bacterial infection of my brain or spinal cord. However, he pointed out that his well-planned diagnostic studies confirmed that I had a demyelinating disease of my brain and spinal cord called multiple sclerosis (MS). He said that the clinical course of this disease was quite variable. I probably had a relapsing and remitting form of the disease whose course was unpredictable. He indicated there was no way to determine the progression of my illness. Moreover, he emphasized that there was no known treatment or understanding of the cause for this disease. He could administer steroids intravenously to reduce inflammation of my brain and spinal cord, but he hastened to point out that this treatment had not been shown to alter the progression of the illness. Because my symptoms of an impending cold were now completely resolved, he indicated that he would send me home and see me on follow-up visits. He made an appointment for me to see him in his clinic within one month as an out-patient at which time he would answer any further questions, especially those that might impact on my career. He was unsure as to when I could return to work, or return to my professional career as a plastic surgeon. Aware of the complexity and unpredictability of this illness, he would certainly understand if I wanted to go to another neurologist for a second opinion.

On the prescribed date, I returned to the neurologist's office. I had gained considerable strength in my legs, allowing me to walk. Because I still had some weakness in my right leg, I walked with a noticeable limp. His examination demonstrated the persisting hyperactive reflexes in my knees and ankles. He noted that I had considerable difficulty in voluntary movement of my right ankle that resulted in "foot drop," causing me to trip inadvertently when I walked. He explained that I had the relapsing and remitting form of MS. In this form of the illness, I would experience the absence of symptoms for awhile (remissions) and then unexpectedly develop a dramatic worsening of my symptoms (relapse). He indicated that there was no scientific way to determine when my symptoms would worsen or improve. He said that my illness was chronic and the most common neurological disease, affecting more than 400,000 young people in our country.

I asked him the obvious question: "How can I get stronger?" His simple prescription was, "Don't do too much and don't do too little." He said to me that I should consider his office door always open to me, inviting me to return whenever I wanted. However, he was not going to make a return appointment. I was surprised by his decision to have no follow-up visit. However, I did not search for an explanation as I believed that he viewed his role in patient care as a diagnostician, rather than a doctor involved in rehabilitation. Because we had no Department of Rehabilitation Medicine, I guess he felt he had no one to whom to refer me. As I left the office, I knew that I had a new *goal* in my career: *to develop a modern rehabilitation program for patients with MS*. When my planned rehabilitation program would allow me to return to work, my next *goal* was to *cure MS*.

My illness was confusing to my colleagues for several reasons. First, there was a justifiable concern that my failure to perform surgery would cause considerable financial hardship to the Department of Plastic Surgery. Consequently, the following comment from my colleague, "If you stay, you may bankrupt the department," while unduly harsh and pessimistic, did not offend me as deeply as one might think. I understood his perspective. Second, my disease must have reminded my colleagues of their own mortality. Comments like, "MS – that kills you pretty quickly, doesn't it?", provided insight into their subconscious fear of death. This initial feeling of doom and gloom surrounding my illness was resolved by the Dean of the medical school, Dr. Norman Knorr, who was a compassionate human being and able to predict accurately the integrity and potential of faculty. Because I had a proven track record with my development of an emergency medical system in Virginia as well as the creation of a burn and trauma center, he believed that I could continue to be an asset to our medical center. He predicted correctly that my disability would enhance my skills as a physician and provide a new direction for leadership in the medical school. Consequently, he secured sufficient funds to allow me to continue my professional career (rather than be placed on disability) and answer the question, "Can a Crip be a contributor to a medical school?"

Rehabilitation Program for Patients with MS

My therapeutic approach to my own illness has been twofold: 1) to develop an effective rehabilitation program and 2) to cure my illness. My rehabilitation program has three distinct components: muscle strengthening and cardiac conditioning, adaptive and assisted living, and accessibility to society. I thought that muscle strengthening and cardiac conditioning would be easy to achieve even though I still had weakness in my legs. I purchased a stationary exercise bicycle and started my muscle-strengthening program. While I anticipated that my bicycle workout would result in some fatigue, I was shocked to find that it left me with profound weakness in my legs. I was so frightened by the experience that I discontinued this standard approach to muscle strengthening. Why did exercise exhaust me? I found the answer in the medical literature, learning that muscle strength and cardiac conditioning are especially challenging *goals* to achieve in the MS patient because the nerves in the brain and spinal cord have lost their myelin coating. Normal myelinated nerves maintain normal conduction until the body temperature reaches over 44°C. When the temperature is elevated, nerve conduction will slow. In the MS patient with demyelinated nerves, even a slight increase in temperature can cause interruption of nerve conduction.

I was also surprised that the adverse effects of elevated core temperature on the neurological signs and symptoms of MS have been well known for more than 50 years.[1] It was understood that patients with MS experience worsening of their neurologic deficits with exercise and other states of hyperthermia. These phenomena form the basis for the hot bath test that aided in the diagnosis of MS. During this test, the induced hyperthermia provided the appearance of new signs and symptoms, indicating the presence of one or more previously unrecognized silent lesions in the brain and spinal cord.

There is, however, growing evidence that significant elevation of body temperature in patients with MS is risky, either precipitating permanent neurological deficit or exposing the patient to circumstances that may predispose them to serious injury. Following self-immersion in a hot bath, use of a hairdryer, or sunbathing, patients with MS experienced neurological changes, some of which were irreversible. With the advent of new diagnostic tests (nuclear magnetic resonance imaging, evoked potential, etc.), the hot bath test has been discontinued in recent years as a means for establishing the diagnosis. It was surprising to find recently that a neurologist at the University of Virginia Hospital was still using the hot bath test to diagnose MS in his patients. One of his residents had positioned a young medical student with MS in a bathtub filled with hot water, watching to see its adverse effects. When the patient's condition worsened to such a degree that he began to sink into the water, he was quickly removed from the tub by an attendant. When I asked the neurologist why his resident was performing this test, he answered with a smile, "She was just having some fun, watching to see what would happen." As I grew accustomed to my new role as physician-as-patient, I was constantly surprised to witness the defense mechanisms adopted by people working in healthcare. Cloaking issues of morality in humor seems to be the most popular device.

I soon realized that this elevation of core body temperature induced by exercise could be prevented if the patient with MS exercised in cool water.[2] After reporting our findings in a medical journal, several manufacturers of temperature-controlled exercise pools offered to donate one of their pools to our University's rehabilitation program. Because we had no Department of Rehabilitation Medicine, a committee consisting of physicians and physical therapists considered the value of this generous gift. Because the water temperature could be adjusted, it could be used by MS patients as well as other individuals. They declined the offer because there was no physical therapist employed at the University who was able to swim!

Realizing the benefits of this aquatic exercise program, the first MS exercise pool was built in our home and opened on November 26, 1985. I was indeed surprised by the interest of MS patients in using our pool. It was occupied all day, five days per week. After NBC's *Today* televised this new concept in rehabilitation, visitors from all over the country came to our home to use the pool.

Opening our home to patients with MS was a fortuitous opportunity to meet many kind and compassionate individuals concerned about this disease. One individual, Charles Ross, changed my life during his visits to my home. Like me, Charles had developed MS at the peak of his very successful business career with Merrill Lynch. This illness clearly interrupted his previously assured ascendancy within his company. Charles had a profound influence on my life. He was able to identify the untapped potential in young people and referred many promising students to me at the University. Because these students had a wide range of interests, I enjoyed seeing their academic contributions to the different schools within our University.

Charles was a charismatic individual who developed close friendships with many visionary business leaders. Charles introduced me to many of these individuals whom he believed would bring new perspectives to my academic career. His friends, Jack McCrane and Chris Hendersen, took a special interest in the University of Virginia and strengthened the relationship between the business community and University scientists by establishing the University of Virginia Inventor of the Year Award. This award recognizes one scientist per year whose patent has resulted in a successful partnership between the University and a specific company. Since its establishment, the rate at which scientists have applied for patents has nearly doubled, benefiting the scientist, the University, industry, and the consumer.

Charles was a superb business person who knew how to inspire people to get a job done. Because he understood my plans to develop a modern rehabilitation program for patients with MS, he became a generous contributor to our research investigations. He graciously enlisted the support of his friends to join in our dream of curing MS. During our joint efforts to cure MS, his wife, Beth, became a strong and eloquent supporter of our efforts. Most importantly, Charles grew to be one of my best friends as we shared our victories and defeats in battling this great crippler of young people. His untimely death in 1994 in a house fire was a tremendous personal loss to me. It has been indeed fortunate for me that I have been able to share my grief for his loss with his wife, Beth, and daughter, Megan, who have patiently allowed me to reflect on the fond memories of our friendship.

Because our small pool could not meet the demands of the numerous patients in our community, we tried to enlist the help of the Charlottesville Department of Recreation, which is in charge of public pools. When one of our undergraduate students, Bob Zura, visited the public pools, he was surprised to find that the water in many of the pools was dirty and unfit for swimming.[3] Pool maintenance was not achieved in a uniform and safe way because our state health department had no sanitary code for the pools. That year, we successfully passed a bill in the state legislature that mandated the Department of Health to establish such a code. With the implementation of this code, the city's pools were now safe for all individuals, including patients with MS. Realizing the need for well-trained physicians in rehabilitation medicine, I enlisted again the help of Vice-President of the Health Sciences Center, Dr. William H. Muller, to develop a separate Department of Rehabilitation Medicine. Dr. Muller saw the merits of such a department and successfully championed its development.

The use of hypothermia, or cold water, to maintain the core body temperature during exercise has gained wide acceptance by physicians treating patients with MS throughout the country. For those who enjoy swimming, relatively inexpensive temperature-controlled exercise pools have been designed to allow one to swim against a current of water or exercise in a standing position, using hydrofitness devices. For those who cannot swim or do not enjoy being in the water, vests and caps have been developed that cool these body parts during exercise. These cooling devices are manufactured by several companies and are available to individuals with MS.

Despite the success of this aquatic exercise program, there was a progression in my illness that caused me to develop considerable expertise in identifying and even designing new assistive devices. You can appreciate that, progressing from a cane to a walker, motorized scooter, and then a stand-up wheelchair, I was benefiting from these adaptive devices. I transfer from my bed and toilet using Barrier-Free lifts. I have helped design a Maine antigravity vest that can be attached to this lift and simplifies dressing. I use a Hi-Rider wheelchair that allows me to stand and dance when I use the chair. This wheelchair gives me an ominous posture of a seven-foot giant. It has considerably changed my perspective. Using the conventional wheelchair, I had to gaze up at people. Now, I look down on them. More importantly, it takes pressure off my buttocks. This wheelchair fits securely in the tie-down system of my new, candy-apple red Braun Entervan Dodge Caravan from Mid-Atlantic Mobility, allowing me to drive through uncharted territories.[4] The floor of the van is automatically lowered as a remote-controlled ramp ascends to the ground. Furthermore, I developed an external condom catheter system that allows urine to be collected in a bag rather than saturating my clothes.[5] While this system is a hybrid, put together with different components from various manufacturers, I am enlisting the help of one manufacturer to sell this improved urine collection system. I have lost much of the spontaneity of living, having to depend on the assistance of others. I see myself following in the large footsteps of the gifted scientist, Stephen Hawking, an individual with amyotrophic lateral sclerosis, who continues to be a world-renowned physicist.

With persistent business travel as well as work at the University, I realized that continuation of my professional career would depend on finding personal care assistance. For individuals without disability, finding a personal care assistant would appear to be easily achieved. In my experiences, finding the right individual has been a challenging experience. One would think that agencies would be adept at matching a personal care assistant to the most appropriate position, but I have found that this is not the case. I have been far more successful in finding dynamic individuals on my own. The four most important job requirements for my personal care assistant in my home are: that the individual can benefit personally from the professional relationship, that there be mutual respect, that the individual have dreams and a desire to grow both personally and professionally, and that he or she demonstrates self-awareness and a desire to interact with the world. One would believe that a person satisfying these requirements would ultimately leave the position for new, challenging opportunities after a relatively short period of time (i.e., one year). While I would be saddened to see such an individual leave, I would celebrate and try to make possible their new opportunities. Whatever the time interval, I consider this experience with an alive, dynamic human being to be far more beneficial than a lifelong arrangement with an emotionally dead healthcare worker whose life begins after work.

One might expect that an experienced healthcare worker would have considerable experience in assisting individuals with a disability. In my opinion, most healthcare workers, including doctors, nurses, certified nursing assistants, physical therapists, and occupational therapists, are not trained to assist effectively in these simple activities of daily life. For example, I have counted only one nurse in our hospital who is able to reliably put on an external condom catheter for urine collection. For lifting, the hospital relies on muscular giants to transfer patients. For the average-sized healthcare worker who will be susceptible to back injuries after transferring patients, our hospital does not require back support braces for all hospital employees involved in patient lifting. Consequently, patient transfer is still an occupational hazard. Moreover, the staff is embarrassed when dealing with body excretions. The invariably female nurse who is skilled in removing fecal impactions from the constipated patient has been inappropriately recognized by colleagues as the "bowel queen."

On July 26, 1990, society suddenly became accessible to persons with disabilities. The American with Disabilities Act (ADA) was signed into law by President Bush and is heralded as the "Emancipation Proclamation for the Disabled" by its advocates.[6] The ADA went beyond previous legislation by requiring a broad array of accommodations and rights for the disabled and guaranteed equal opportunities for persons with disabilities in employment, state and local government services, public accommodations, transportation, and telecommunications. I first recognized the power of the ADA when Jason Hintz, a third-year undergraduate student, came into my office. He was already a mature disabled rights activist who knew what he was talking about. He told me in one simple sentence words that changed my life and became a *life-defining experience*: "Persons who discriminate more than any other group against disabled people are physicians." Because I had taken considerable pride in viewing myself as a patient's rights advocate, I challenged Jason to prove it to me. He welcomed me to be *present in the moment* to a tour of our hospital that was a sickening experience. We visited every bathroom in our ambulatory care center and found that none were accessible to persons with disabilities. I had been treating patients in wheelchairs and never asked the simple question: "Can you use our bathroom to urinate or defecate?" I'm afraid that their answer would have been, "I do it in my pants at the University of Virginia Hospital." Embarrassed by my ignorance about the issue, I had devised a new goal: *make the University of Virginia Hospital accessible to persons with disabilities*. I immediately took Jason to the head of the hospital and described the numerous architectural barriers in our hospital. I demanded that the hospital eliminate all of them in accordance with the ADA. After spending approximately $3 million, our hospital is one of the few in the country that is accessible to persons with disabilities. When I designed our new 16-bed burn and wound healing center, all architectural barriers to persons with disabilities were eliminated so that persons with disabilities could work or be cared for in this facility.[7]

The hospital's immediate willingness to make these extensive renovations is due, in part, to the University's nationally recognized commitment to students with disabilities. Spearheaded by the eloquent spokesperson for students with disabilities, Patricia Lampkin, Vice President of Student Affairs, the University of Virginia had already made Thomas Jefferson's historic academic village accessible to persons with disabilities without significantly altering the beauty of this international landmark. Realizing that the University was proud of its accomplishments in complying with the ADA, the hospital had little choice but to follow in Patricia Lampkin's vision of accessibility.

I continued to be amazed that the private and federal agencies that accredit hospitals do not search for architectural barriers in their review. The Joint Commission of Hospital Accreditation as well as the Healthcare Finance Administration do not consider accessibility as part of their review process and leave the responsibility up to a Department of Justice overwhelmed with complaints. My advocacy for the ADA has extended into the business communities throughout the country. I have filed successful complaints to the Department of Justice that have caused the following businesses and schools to remove barriers: Newark Airport, Charlotte Airport, Schubert Theater (New York), Mcleod Hotel (New York) and Trinity School (New York). These successful petitions occurred soon after passage of the ADA when the Department of Justice's eight attorneys were just beginning to deal with complaints. Since passage of the ADA, these attorneys have been inundated with complaints and have turned a deaf ear to my letters and telephone calls. After my first successful efforts to ensure compliance with the ADA, the Department of Justice attorneys have not filed another complaint for me. In the absence of their help, the government attorneys suggested that I hire my own attorney to file these complaints and pay for my private attorney's legal fees. This recommendation is irrefutable evidence that the federal government does not have adequate staff to enforce the ADA.

Cure MS

My next *goal*, to cure MS, has not yet been accomplished. I attribute this delay in a large part to my lack of focus on this project. I subconsciously feared that science was not sophisticated enough to cure my illness, and so I focused my energy on more practically applied projects dealing with rehabilitation. When I expanded my research program searching for a cure for my illness, I was surprised to find that there were well-trained scientists who had considerable experience in studying the cause of diseases like MS. In 1978, scientists had identified the first retrovirus that caused a disease identical to MS! A virus is a microscopic particle composed of a core of ribonucleic acid (RNA) or deoxyribonucleic acid (DNA) that is surrounded by a protein coat and unable to replicate without a host. A retrovirus is a virus that has its genetic blueprint only in the form of RNA; it must therefore employ an enzyme such as reverse transcriptase (found in HIV) to translate its RNA into DNA before it can replicate within the host. The HIV is the retrovirus that causes AIDS.

The retrovirus causing a disease indistinguishable from multiple sclerosis was called human T-cell lymphotropic virus-I (HTLV-I). Its discovery laid the groundwork for identifying the related virus that causes AIDS.[8] AIDS was first recognized in the United States in the summer of 1981. By June 1, 1993, there were 302,000 cumulative cases reported in adults and adolescents in the United States. Approximately 60 percent of that number have died thus far. Today, there are approximately one million HIV-infected people in the United States. AIDS is truly a global pandemic with cases reported from every continent. Because HIV can kill the infected person within five years, scientists focused their attention on searching for a treatment and cure of this life-threatening infection, overlooking the chronic neurologic disease caused by HTLV-I.

HTLV-I is structurally linked to a number of chronic diseases, namely, HTLV-associated myelopathy or tropical spastic paraparesis (HAM/ TSP) as well as adult T-cell leukemia/ lymphoma. It has also been identified as an important causal factor in specific autoimmune diseases, such as uveitis (inflammation of the middle layer of the eye), polymyositis (muscles inflammation) and arthritis (joint inflammation). One can estimate that the lifelong risk of infected individuals to develop an HTLV-associated disease is approximately five percent. HAM/TSP is a demyelinating disease of the spinal cord and brain that is identical to the chronic progressive form of MS and is found predominantly in the Caribbean, some areas of Africa, southwestern Japan and Italy. The major routes of HTLV-I transmission are perinatal, transmission occurs predominantly postnatally through breast feeding; parenterally (through blood transfusion or exposure to needles and syringes contaminated with blood) and sexually. Because we live in a global world with easy air transportation, it should come as no surprise that 1%-2% of our population now carry this retrovirus. The number of HTLV-I infected individuals is estimated to be 25 million.

Knowing the successful treatment of AIDS, we may think that there have been similar advances in the treatment of HAM/TSP. Because there has been negligible research support to find a treatment for this "chronic disease," none has been identified. Fortunately, the number of HTLV-I infected individuals, together with the severity of associated diseases, has recently caught the attention of scientists in France who have received limited funding to develop a vaccine to prevent this retroviral infection. Preventative clinical trials may involve intravenous drug users in the industrialized world who still have not been infected by this retrovirus. These therapeutic vaccine trials in intravenous drug users should protect them against disease development. If we could learn how this retrovirus demyelinates the brain, then we could identify drug therapies to prevent it. In the very least, we should be able to develop a vaccine to prevent the illnesses caused by this retrovirus.[9,10]

How does this HTLV-I retrovirus affect you, the reader? If you have a chronic disease, like MS, leukemia, arthritis, uveitis or polymyositis, this illness could be caused by the HTLV-I retrovirus. Consequently, you should ask your physician to test your blood for this retrovirus. If the test confirms that you have an HTLV-I induced chronic illness, you will learn that there is no treatment for this disease. In addition, the physician will inform you of methods to prevent the spread of your infectious disease to a loved one: abstaining from sexual relations, practice protected sex, abstain from breastfeeding your infant and avoid giving blood donations.

Americans usually learn that they are asymptomatic carriers of this retrovirus when they are planning to donate blood. Because blood banks do not accept blood from donors with HTLV-I, blood donors are routinely screened for this retrovirus. When an asymptomatic carrier is identified, blood bank directors then provide counseling to the carrier of HTLV-I. First, the blood bank director indicates to the HTLV-I carrier that this information will be kept confidential, so it will not become part of the patient's medical records. In addition, the blood bank director will not report this information to the donor's primary care physician, state health department or Centers for Disease Control. The blood bank director will then advise the individual on recommended techniques to prevent spreading this retrovirus. The blood bank director usually comforts the patient with the information that the diseases caused by this retrovirus are chronic diseases. I remember one blood bank director telling these asymptomatic carriers that HTLV-I induced chronic diseases are not like AIDS, which kills patients in a short period of time. The blood bank director then gives some more good news to the asymptomatic HTLV-I carrier: he or she only has a 5% chance of developing one of these chronic diseases. The HTLV-I carrier will ask the obvious questions about the implications of this infectious disease on insurance, disability and employment applications. Some blood bank directors have told me they have advised individuals to lie on these applications in order to avoid denial of their application for health coverage and employment. The Centers for Disease Control, as well as the State Health Departments, join in this conspiracy of silence by concealing the incidence of this infectious disease. Failure to report the frequency of this infectious disease is an invitation to a global epidemic of fatal chronic illnesses. It is inconceivable to me how the medical profession could be a facilitator of this global epidemic.

Realizing the potential therapeutic implications of studies of HTLV-I, I had to find a microbiologist at the University of Virginia who could direct this program. To achieve this *goal*, my daughter, Elizabeth, raised $125,000 to endow a chair in the Microbiology Department for a distinguished scientist who would lead this research program. Dr. Thomas Parsons, the recipient of this endowed chair, has coordinated a comprehensive scientific program that examines the role of retroviruses in the development of MS, AIDS, as well as cancer. Dr. Parsons is a recognized virologist, who has been instrumental in demonstrating that viruses cause cancer in humans and animals. After his appointment as Chairman of the Department of Microbiology, he was instrumental in recruiting Dr. Marie-Louise Hammarskjöld and her husband, Dr. David Rekosh, who were able to examine the damaging effects of human retroviruses on the nervous system.

Using the generous financial support of my friend Charles Ross and his wonderful friends, the Charles H. Ross, Jr., Endowed Chair for Multiple Sclerosis Research was then established. Following discussions with Charles, Dr. Hammerskjöld agreed to accept this leadership position. After Drs. Hammarskjöld and Rekosh established their large comprehensive retroviral laboratory, they attracted two additional talented scientists, Dr. Oliver John Semmes and Dr. Bernhard Maier, whose research focused entirely on the retroviral infections that cause neurological diseases that are identical to MS.

After seeking the advice of Augusto Odone, I am expending considerable personal effort toward curing my disease, taking a hint from his journey. In September 1998, we held the first Charles H. Ross, Jr., Human Lymphotrophic Retroviral Research Symposium, searching for a cure for HAM/TSP. This conference was attended by renowned scientists with considerable expertise in HTLV-I research. This symposium was sponsored by the Charles Edison Fund and was attended by three members of its board, John Keegan, Dr. John Schullinger and Robert Murray. Beth Ross and I participated in the discussions to help focus the symposium. Drs. Maier and Hammarskjöld have successfully developed an animal model in which this retrovirus causes a neurologic disease. If we can find drug therapies that cure these diseased animals, these same therapies should help patients with this form of MS as well as other types of MS. This concentrated, multidisciplinary inquiry focusing on HTLV-I will proceed at an exponentially accelerating pace. Subsequently, I predict that most forms of MS will be referred to as retroviral diseases.

This shift from defining the disease as the loss of myelin around the nerve to identifying the specific infective agent will reflect a fundamental change in thinking, focusing on the cause rather than on the tissues seen under the microscope.

Because modern science has now identified one cause of MS, it would seem to be a relatively simple task to find a cure to this retroviral infection, such as the one being achieved with the AIDS retrovirus. Sufficient funds must now be raised or allocated to achieve this *goal*. I am saddened to tell you that it is very difficult to achieve the dream of curing a chronic illness because of medicine and society's view of chronic illnesses. They view fallaciously that chronic illness is incurable. Unknowingly, the medical profession sees positive and negative aspects of such illnesses. With considerable embarrassment, I believe that some physicians view chronic illness to be an important revenue-generator. In many cases, the treatment of such illnesses is the life-blood of their practice. The importance of a chronic illness to the practicing physician can be best appreciated by reflecting on a conference I attended for all urology residents around the country. The topic of the lecture was benign prostatic hypertrophy (BPH), a condition that affects the majority of males beyond the age of 50. As the male ages, his prostate will enlarge and obstruct the outflow of urine. This obstruction is corrected by a surgical procedure done by a urologist. The lecturer began his talk by saying, "I have some good news and some bad news about benign prostatic hypertrophy. The good news is that scientists are gaining new understandings about the causes of this disease that affects most men. The bad news is that we are not close to a cure." At that moment, the residents responded with a thunderous applause. I must confess that I was shocked by their inappropriate response, causing me to ask one of the residents why he applauded. He responded with a smile saying gleefully, "Surgical treatment of BPH will be 50% of my practice. . .!"

The costs for care of chronic illnesses are so staggering that they could potentially bankrupt society. Considering the present population affected by MS, it has been estimated that the total cost to society for the care of these patients during their life will be $133 billion, costing each person in the United States $637.00. If the lifetime costs were annualized, the cost for caring for MS patients is approximately $2 billion per year. The treatment of other more common chronic illnesses has an even bigger price tag! Diabetes mellitus, affecting more than 10 million Americans, is the most common cause of blindness, amputations, and kidney failure. The estimated annual cost for caring for these individuals is $20 billion. The most common chronic illness is aging, a fact that surprises most physicians as well as society. Because aging affects every one of us with signs of graying hair, wrinkled skin, and progressive loss of muscle strength, it is considered by most as a "normal" process, rather than a disease entity. Modern scientists realize that aging is, in fact, a disease that is probably due to our body's progressive loss of its ability to regenerate tissue parts. When a young child's finger is amputated above the cuticle on the nail, the child will regenerate a normal nail and fingertip like a lizard regrowing its tail. After the age of ten, the child loses its ability to regenerate the fingertip and heals instead with a thick scar. Aging occurs by scar tissue that smothers the regenerating cells in our tissue. The cost of healthcare for the elderly likely exceeds $200 billion per year.

In light of the enormous economic implications to society, it is important to consider the magnitude and source of funding for research that will lead to the identification of the causes of these chronic diseases as well as to find a cure. The total healthcare research budget in our country is $35.8 billion. Private medical companies spend $18.645 billion for medical research, a funding source that exceeds the $15.8 billion research budget allocated by the federal government. Private and nonprofit foundations provide an additional $1.3 billion for medical research. Despite the enormous cost and suffering of chronic and acute disease to our society, the allocation of resources for research in medicine are considerably less than in other sectors of our society. Only 3.5% of the total healthcare budget is allocated to research. In contrast, the defense complex in our country wisely allocates 14.8% of its budget to develop innovative approaches to defend our country. Private industry companies, like Microsoft, ensure that our country is competitive in our global economy and spend approximately 16% of their funds for research.

The limited federal funding for medical research has several important implications. Most importantly, it has created an academic research environment that no longer attracts the brightest candidates. Students are reluctant to pursue a career in which there is fierce competition for research funding. Today, scientists have to compete aggressively for this relatively small level of funding, realizing that only one of four grants will be approved. Consequently, the investigations of most scientists are frequently interrupted because of the lack of funding.

The scarcity of research funds has caused many special interest groups to develop strategies that successfully alter the allocations of National Institutes of Health's (NIH) research funds. Medical science has now become a political arena in which the "favorite diseases" are designated by these special interest groups. The inequities of the allocation of research spending can be appreciated by determining the research dollars spent for the cure of individual persons afflicted: aging, $.25 per person; diabetes mellitus, $20 per person; multiple sclerosis, $30 per person; Parkinson's disease, $34 per person; heart disease, $74 per person; Alzheimer's disease, $81 per person; breast cancer, $200 per person; cancer, $338 per person; and HIV/AIDS, $2,143 per person.

Today, there is a growing realization that federal funding for medical research must be dramatically increased. Support for biomedical research has become a bipartisan issue in 1998 as Republican and Democratic leaders and the President have agreed that the budget for the NIH should be doubled by the year 2003. In his State of the Union address in January 1998, President Clinton asked for an increase of $1.15 billion, or 8.5% next year. In addition, he called for an increase of about 50% over the next years, raising the agency's budget to more than $20 billion in 2003.

Congressman John Edward Porter, Republican of Illinois, who is chairman of the appropriations subcommittee responsible for biomedical research, and other members of Congress, have publicly supported the *goal* of doubling the spending for the NIH in the next five years. The Ad Hoc Group for Medical Research Funding, a diverse coalition of nearly 200 patient and voluntary health groups, medical and scientific societies, academic and research organizations and industry has proposed a 15% increase in funding for the NIH for fiscal year 1999 as the first step toward the *goal* of doubling the NIH budget.

A national outreach campaign, NIH², has been started to generate and nurture public support for increasing the NIH budget. NIH² is in part the brain child of Morton Kondracke, a Washington, D.C. journalist and policy pundit, who became involved with the Parkinson's Action Network, a disease-specific lobbying organization, because his wife has Parkinson's disease. His frustration over the comparatively low level of funding for Parkinson's research rapidly turned into a realization that any effort to increase support would require competing directly with other diseases, such as AIDS and cancer. He quickly concluded that the only way to get more for Parkinson's disease was to double the whole.

Prescription for Curing

Double NIH funding.

The most obvious solution to the problem of curing MS and other chronic illnesses would be for the federal government to double the funding for the National Institutes of Health. Consequently, we must urge our legislators and President to implement this simple solution.

Lobby the President and Congress to allocate $2 billion annually in NIH funding to cure MS.

Because every person in our country knows a person with MS or has MS, you must write the President, your Congressmen and Senator and demand that $2 billion in NIH funding be allocated each year to cure MS. Because local representatives determine the importance of a problem by the size of the stack of letters, everyone must write a letter to Congress.

Special interest groups committed to curing MS must monitor carefully the research projects at NIH.

The public has a right to review NIH's plan to cure MS. Its plan must include a timetable to end this curable chronic illness.

Develop a scientific hypothesis that can lead to a cure of MS.

Given the current climate in our country in which there is inadequate research funding, I have been compelled to develop a privately funded, fiscally responsible plan through which I will be able to cure my own illness. We are achieving these scientific postulates with the HTLV-1 retrovirus that causes a form of MS. Scientific investigations of the HTLV-1 retrovirus fulfill many of Koch's postulates that are needed to demonstrate that an organism is responsible for a specific disease.

1. HTLV-1 retrovirus has been shown to be present in all humans suffering from HAM/TSP and is found in some healthy human beings.
2. The HTLV-1 retrovirus has been isolated from individuals with HAM/TSP and grown in pure culture on artificial laboratory media.
3. This freshly isolated HTLV-1 retrovirus, when inoculated into a healthy laboratory animal, causes the same disease seen in human beings.

4. The HTLV-1 retrovirus can be reisolated in pure culture from the experimental infection.

Identify scientists who are recognized authorities in the field.

Most authorities who have expertise in HTLV-1 infections have been identified.

Convene an international conference with the world's leading authorities who can develop a plan to cure the disease, establish a time frame, and raise the moneys needed.

In September 1998, these scientists attended the three-day Charles H. Ross, Jr., Human Lymphotrophic Virus Symposium to design the scientific plan to cure this form of MS. This meeting included some individuals who have MS or have an affected family member.

Develop a business plan that outlines strategies for curing the disease and contact individuals who are willing to financially support this program.

I realize now that our small dedicated scientific team will never cure my illness. Two experienced scientists and one postdoctoral fellow are not sufficient person power to create a comprehensive scientific program to cure MS. I need to raise $250 million to support a modern dynamic research program that will cure my disease in a five-year to ten-year time interval. Consequently, I am asking for the generous support of wealthy visionaries who want to cure chronic illnesses. There are several important implications to curing MS. First, the cure will benefit the 400,000 people with this disease. In addition, curing MS will serve as a model of hope for curing other chronic illnesses, like diabetes mellitus, rheumatoid arthritis, aging, Parkinson's disease, etc. Who is going to answer my call for help?

I believe that the noted fashion designer, Oscar de la Renta, would be an ideal donor for this research program in memory of his beloved mother who died of MS. Perhaps Richard Pryor, the comic genius, who suffers from MS would want to be the financial benefactor. Annette Funicello, the Hollywood star who has multiple sclerosis, could spearhead this program. Jeff Grayson, an individual with multiple sclerosis, would be an ideal business man to coordinate our program. Jeff is a business owner and philanthropist who started Capitol Consultants in 1968. His firm specializes in financial management and manages assets in excess of $1 billion.

Other individuals come to mind who realize the importance of changing the culture of our planet. Ted Turner, the founder of Cable News Network (CNN), could easily recognize the benefits to humanity of curing chronic illnesses in focused research programs. The master computer scientist, Bill Gates, could change the world of medical care as he revolutionizes global communication. Warren Buffet, the financial wizard, could guide us to success in curing illnesses. Oprah Winfrey could bring hope to patients with MS who had lost hope. The noted author, John Grisham, a resident of Charlottesville, could champion this program from his home. Tom Cruise and Sissy Spacek, other Charlottesville residents, would be welcome additions to our team. The Dave Matthews Band could sing our cause to the world. A respected foundation, like the Merrill Lynch Foundation or the Pew Charitable Trusts, could take this leadership role. My most important message to each of them is that I desperately need your help to change an old paradigm of medical care about incurable diseases and demonstrate to the world that well-supported focused research can cure diseases and change our lives.

The scientists should complete research reports semiannually to update the donors.

In April 1999, we will publish our first report that will be included in a Website and distributed to interested individuals as well as donors.

An interested individual should meet with the scientists each month to monitor the program's progress.

I will meet with these scientists in an effort to celebrate their advances in curing MS.

The blueprint for NIH^2 requires lobbying with the mobilizations of existing organizations. The plan also calls for the launch of "America's Campaign for Medical Research," featuring public service announcements and paid advertisements to reach the general public. Kondracke has enlisted the support of a Washington, D.C. public relations firm, Fleishman-Hillard, Inc., which is now involved in planning NIH^2.

The architects of NIH^2 say their effort is geared to work only in the short term, while other initiatives, such as Research America's 435 project, will conduct long-term advocacy efforts. Research America, a national nonprofit alliance, formed to raise the profile of medical research, initially launched its grass roots campaign in six targeted areas. Presently, it has a full-time staff funded by a budget that exceeds $1 million. It is slated for eventual expansion into each of the nation's 435 Congressional districts. Like NIH^2, Project 435's first *goal* is to double the NIH budget, but it also seeks to establish a national network of activists to head off any future challenges to biomedical research.

The successes of the special interest groups championing a cure for HIV/AIDS have drawn an accurate picture of this epidemic that affects literally every member of this planet. It has made undeniable requests for the development of treatments for this life-threatening infection as well as a vaccine that will prevent the illness. It has carefully orchestrated advocacy groups that wear emblems reminiscent of the disease and include notoriety from Hollywood stars, who eloquently urge society to cure this dreadful disease. Its approach to fund-raising has become a model for all special interest groups. Perceiving the success of raising moneys for HIV/AIDS research, one could argue that all special interest groups should use this same approach to raise sufficient funds to cure their disease. Appreciating the urgency of the mission to cure each disease entity, these advocacy groups can serve as a valuable conscience that oversees the research projects and ensures that they are focused and designed to cure disease.

In the absence of adequate federal funding, charities have been formed in this search for cures for disease.[11] Unfortunately, the existence of charities soothes our collective conscience, giving us the unfounded confidence that science is near a cure. Many of these ill-managed organizations are staffed by an army of fund-raisers whose salaries account for 50% to 90% of their operating budgets. These charities raise money by frightening individuals with chronic illnesses with high-budget, "high-drama" advertising. The charities explain their use of these advertising tactics as an effort to gain the public's attention, which they feel is already saturated with other like organizations' campaigns. Smothered in the weeds of bureaucracy, charities are ineffectual in developing a focused research program designed to find *cures* for these chronic diseases in a well-defined time interval. In the light of their limited funding, as well as federal funding for research, the charities should become lean, mean operating machines that lobby successfully for dramatic increases in federal research support to cure chronic diseases. Once the chronic disease is cured, the charity should redirect its efforts, searching for a cure of another chronic disease.

Today, the federal government will only spend sufficient moneys to cure a disease if the disease has the following characteristics. First, the disease must rapidly spread to young individuals throughout the world. Second, a large number of the young people who become afflicted with the disease must die in a short period of time, five years to ten years. Polio and HIV are the best examples of these life-threatening disease epidemics that frighten the world. In contrast, illnesses that kill individuals within a short time interval, zero to 30 days, do not spread rapidly and are ignored by society. Similarly, chronic illnesses, like aging, MS and diabetes mellitus, cause long-term disability that is also overlooked.

The polio and AIDS epidemics have fostered miraculous scientific adventures that are leading to cures of these dreaded diseases. With the development of the polio vaccine, polio has disappeared from most of the world, except in India and Africa. The Rotary Club International (PolioPlus Partners) has raised $1 billion to eliminate polio from these last two regions where the disease continues to persist. Because of global travel, we must continue to spend the annual $100 million needed to immunize our children against the disease. When polio disappears completely, this money spent for immunization of our children will be saved.

With a budget of $2 billion per year supported by the federal government, scientists are having the same success with efforts to cure the AIDS epidemic. When the epidemic was first identified in the early 1980s, it was viewed as a fatal illness that would kill infected individuals within a period of seven years. With the development of triple drug therapy, patients infected with HIV can be effectively treated. AIDS is now viewed as a chronic illness. The development of the vaccine is on the horizon.

In this chapter, I have summarized some of the *profiles for success* in curing illnesses as prescriptions for curing your illness. Reading these prescriptions should empower you to join with other healthcare workers through uncharted waters. It is my hope that the outcome of your journey will bring relief to you as well as other human beings.

8

Lover's Search

"Healers must understand that love does not only mean love for others; it also means love for oneself. We must be aware of our limits and know when it is necessary to nurture ourselves. We must strike a balance between what we do for ourselves and what we do for others, learning to receive as well as to give."
Elisabeth Kübler-Ross

The quickest way for a surgeon to realize his mortality is to develop an illness that is so severe that he becomes unwelcome in the operating room. My initial approaches to avoid dealing with my own mortality were to become an expert in adaptive living and begin the search for the cause and cure of my illness, MS. Armed with my Ph.D. in denial, these efforts kept my mind busy in my search for eternal life. With considerable surprise, I suddenly realized that I was developing an even more serious illness than MS, aging. The earliest sign of this fatal illness was a whitening of the ends of the hairs on my head and eyebrows. An obvious solution to this problem was an immediate surgical removal of any gray hairs. The signs of wrinkling of the skin around my eyes, crow's feet, and lips were a much more ominous sign of this dreaded disease. Being a plastic surgeon, recognized for being victorious over wrinkles in my patients, my male ego needs were too great to gain the benefits of eyelid surgery and a facelift. I thought that there was a separate and less expensive approach to dealing with the most common cause of death that suited my intellectual approach to problem-solving, learning about death and dying.

In my initial search for experts in this field, I fantasized that I would have to travel to distant lands to talk with either the Dalai Lama or, perhaps, the Pope. It was like a gift from heaven that I was able to cancel my reservations to Thailand and Rome because Dr. Elisabeth Kübler-

Ross had just moved to a 320-acre farm in Highland County, the least populated county east of the Mississippi and a mere 120 miles from my home. I immediately called her office in Head Waters, Virginia, and made an appointment to meet her at her farm. Her secretary thought I might enjoy attending one of her upcoming workshops on Life, Death and Transition. My immediate response to her thoughtful suggestion was that the five-day workshop was far too long for a busy surgeon; moreover, the workshop seemed to cover other areas that would interfere with my focus on death and dying. Realizing that I had made my mind up with insufficient information, she transferred my call to Dr. Kübler-Ross' home.

I knew immediately that I was speaking to Dr. Kübler-Ross when I heard her soft voice. Her notable Swiss accent provided some authority to her kind invitation to join her for lunch at her home. When I explained that I used a wheelchair, she immediately responded that we would have lunch on the patio beneath the cover of the trees surrounding her home. Having lunch with Dr. Kübler-Ross was a unique opportunity for me because I, like millions of others, had read her classic book, *On Death and Dying*. The publication of that book revolutionized medicine's treatment of dying patients by being instrumental in the launching of the hospice movement in the United States, helping to transform the medical profession's attitudes toward a concept considered to be taboo, and giving us descriptions of the stages of dying, which provide a framework for treatment that will continue to endure.

One of the most important psychological studies of the late 20th century, *On Death and Dying*, grew out of Dr. Elisabeth Kübler-Ross' famous interdisciplinary seminar on death and dying.[1] At the beginning of this classic bestseller, Dr. Kübler-Ross looks at the potential consequences of our society's failure to deal with death and dying. "We may want to ask ourselves what happens to man in a society bent on ignoring or avoiding death. . . what happens in the changing field of medicine, where we have to ask ourselves if medicine is to remain a humanitarian and respected profession or a new but depersonalized science in the service of prolonging life rather than diminishing human suffering. Where the medical students have a choice of dozens of lectures on DNA and RNA, but less experience on the simple doctor-patient relationship that used to be the alphabet for every successful family physician. What happens to a society that puts more emphasis on I.Q. and class standards than on simple matters of tact, sensitivity, perceptiveness, and good taste in management of the suffering?" Dr. Kübler-Ross then suggests a solution to this potential depersonalization of the medical profession. " If we could combine the teaching of new scientific and technological achievements with equal emphasis on interpersonal human relationships, we would indeed make progress, but not if the new knowledge is conveyed to the student with less and less interpersonal contact."

In the fall of 1965, four theology students of the Chicago theological seminary approached Dr. Kübler-Ross for assistance in a research project that they had chosen. This research project was to be her *life-defining experience*. Their class was to write a paper on a crisis in human life. The four students considered death as the biggest crisis people had to face. With the assistance of Dr. Elizabeth Kübler-Ross, they searched for an approach to conducting research on dying and realized that the best possible way to study death and dying was to ask terminally ill patients to be their teachers. They planned to observe critically ill patients, study their responses and needs, evaluate the reactions of people around them, and, "get as close to the dying as they would allow us." When they set out to ask physicians if they could interview a terminally ill patient of theirs, their reactions were varied, from stunned looks of disbelief to rather abrupt changes of the topic of conversation.

Dr. Kübler-Ross succinctly commented on the results of her efforts: "I did not get one single chance even to get near one such patient." When she finally found a patient, he welcomed her with open arms, allowing her to be *present in the moment* with the dying patient. When he invited her to sit down, it was obvious that he was eager to speak to Dr. Kübler-Ross. She told him she did not want to hear him now, but would return the next day with her students. With some obvious sadness she said, "I was not sensitive enough to appreciate his communications. It was so hard to get one patient, I had to share him with my students. Little did I realize then that when such a patient says, 'please sit down now,' tomorrow may be too late." When she returned with the students, he was too weak to speak and died less than an hour later. After this first disappointing experience, they seized any opportunity and were able to see a terminally ill patient once a week. In the remaining portion of the book, she summarizes what they had learned from the dying patients and defined the classic stages in dealing with death and dying.

The first stage is denial and isolation: "No, not me, it cannot be true." This first phase gives way to the second stage: anger, "Oh, yes, it is me, it was not a mistake." This second stage is filled with feelings of anger, rage, envy, and resentment. The third stage, the stage of bargaining, is helpful to the patient, but only for brief periods of time. The terminally ill patient knows from past experience that there is a slim chance that he will be rewarded for good behavior. The bargaining is really an attempt to postpone. Many of her patients promised to give parts of their body to science if their doctors used their knowledge of science to extend their lives. The fourth stage, depression, begins when the terminally ill patient can no longer deny his or her illness. The anger and rage are soon replaced with a sense of great loss. All these reasons for depression are well known to each of us; however, Dr. Kübler-Ross points out what we often tend to forget, "The preparatory grief that the terminally ill patient has to undergo in order to prepare himself for the final separation from this world." The final stage is acceptance, at which time, he is neither depressed nor angry about his state. Acceptance should not be mistaken for happiness. Dr. Kübler-Ross explains that acceptance is almost void of feelings. " It is as if the pain had gone, the struggle is over."

After completing her interviews, she summarized briefly what these patients had taught the research group. The outstanding fact is that all the terminally ill patients were aware of the seriousness of their illness, whether they were told or not. There came a time when all patients had a need to share all their concerns, face reality, and take care of important matters while there was still time. She concludes her book with these memorable comments: "Watching a peaceful death of a human being reminds us of a falling star; one of a million lights in a vast sky that flares up for a moment only to disappear into the endless nights forever. To be a therapist to a dying patient makes us aware of the uniqueness of each individual in this vast sea of humanity. It makes us aware of our finiteness, our limited lifespan. Few of us live beyond our three score and ten years and, yet, in that brief time, most of us create and live a unique biography and weave ourselves into the fabric of human history." As she listened to the dying patients, they became her teachers and helped her define one of her life *goals, teach mankind the pathway to living.*

I left Charlottesville at 9 a.m. to allow three hours to travel over the circuitous, mountainous roads to her home in Head Waters. The first 40 miles on route 64 over the Blue Ridge Mountains were easily traveled over a four-lane highway. This modern highway was transformed in Staunton, Virginia, to a two-lane country road leading all the way to Head Waters. Head Waters is a one-building town, featuring an all-in-one post office and general store. Before Dr. Kübler-Ross came to Head

Waters, the post office was open one day per week. With an avalanche of a mail being received daily for the new resident, the postmaster quickly changed the hours of operation to five days per week. Her farm was another four miles from the post office and was easily identified by its sign, Healing Waters Farm.

I found Elisabeth waiting for me in front of her small, white farmhouse, protected by two slobbering Saint Bernard dogs. Her physical appearance came as quite a surprise to me. This giant of medicine was only 5 feet tall, wearing a subdued blouse and skirt. Her sneakers facilitated her quick pace around the farm. The wrinkled skin of her face covered her high cheekbones and encircled her soft, bright eyes. Her broad smile made me feel very comfortable in her modest home. A table and one chair were positioned beneath a tree allowing me to align my wheelchair close to the table. With placemats and silverware on the table, she brought out some homemade quiche. Her first words were: "Welcome to Noah's Ark. My name is Elisabeth. These dogs are the first of my menagerie."

Elisabeth was a gourmet cook. I can assure you that the food was superb. Enjoying good food, especially fresh from her farm, was one of the highlights of her life and a prerequisite for the beginning of a group conversation. Because I was hesitant to discuss the real reason for my visit, to learn more about dying, I thought that I would divert the conversation from this seemingly painful and frightening subject to one that might complement this excellent lunch. I expressed interest in her background and some of the salient features that may have caused her to pursue psychiatry. She responded very comfortably to this question and offered an explanation that she must have delivered to thousands of students. Elisabeth explained that she was the firstborn of triplets born to a middle-class Swiss couple in 1927. "I was independent from the outset. I decided that I would be a physician as a child, much to the confusion and consternation of my successful father who fancied me, if not the perfectly dutiful Swiss housewife, at least the ideal secretary." With a rather serious look, she commented, "When I refused to work for him, he gave me no alternative but to leave home."

Undaunted, she spent years working as a laboratory assistant, struggling to put herself through medical school, as well as traveling extensively throughout war-ravaged Europe as a volunteer. After completing her medical degree in 1957, she furthered her studies in New York after marrying Emanuel Ross, an American neuropathologist. She continued to work in hospitals as she pursued her medical degree, increasingly appalled by the standard treatment of dying patients.

She credited her early experiences, "Viewing the gas chambers, the concentration camps, the train filled with the baby shoes of murdered children, talking with the Jewish girl who had lived through the nightmare of seeing her family march to their deaths," with awakening her to the universal plight of the dying. She realized while still in Europe that people feared death and often painfully clung to life because of what she termed "unfinished business": pent-up emotions like rage, guilt, or grief keeping us from a peaceful end.

After moving to the United States and continuing to witness deathly ill patients being ignored and even abused, she began lecturing the medical profession about everything it was doing wrong. By the time the Rosses moved to Chicago, she was speaking to standing-room only audiences, her lectures featuring patients who simply talked about what they were going through, thereby forcing healthcare professionals to hear them. While her detractors felt her methodology too simple, too absolute amid the messy realities of life and death, all credit her with making the subjects of death and dying accessible and manageable.

Until the publication of her first book in 1969, she pointed out that no one had ever spoken about such issues, much less accused the entire medical profession of failing their patients by not helping them come to terms with death. She provided a simple recommendation: listen to your patients, learn what their concerns are, and help to address them. The publication of *On Death and Dying* and the subsequent feature in *Life* magazine made her an overnight international celebrity. The article, published November 21, 1969, described the work in which Elisabeth was involved, focusing particularly on a young woman with leukemia, Eva. Poignant photographs by McCombe combined with the author Loudon Wainwright's thoughtful and sensitive evaluation of Elisabeth's philosophy and seminars struck a chord worldwide. Immediately, the University of Chicago was flooded with mail and phone calls. Unfortunately, her peers at the University were far less enthused. Accused of being a vulture, of exploiting the emotions of dying patients, the senior professors ordered their faculty and staff to deny Elisabeth access to their dying patients. Any inquiries about Elisabeth were to be handled by the University's public relations office. Finally, reviled and attacked by her own peers, Elisabeth resigned from the University after her seminars were canceled.

After moving with her family to Flossmoor, a suburb outside Chicago, Elisabeth contemplated retiring from public life and opening a manageable practice out of her home with just a few terminally ill patients. But the flood of letters and appeals for her lectures continued to pour in and quelled whatever notions she had of retiring. She began traveling in excess of a quarter of a million miles per year giving lectures and workshops around the country.

In 1970, Elisabeth realized that she could help far more people effectively by meeting with them in groups on a day-to-day basis outside an institutional environment. While she had been lecturing all over the country, reaching about 15,000 people a week, she knew that she was not addressing the problem, merely identifying it. She decided to hold the first of what would be hundreds of Workshops in Life, Death, and Transition, a program she felt would allow people to vent their unfinished business in a safe environment, a place where negativity could be expressed without fear of retribution or disapproval.[2] Initial participants included anyone whose lives had been touched by death: the terminally ill, bereaved, healthcare professionals, clergy, any person involved with the dying. For periods of five days, the groups would meet together and share all meals, during which time they would describe their experiences to one another and learn to vent their emotions. She credits the success of her workshops to her dedicated hand-picked staff, who became creative *powerful problem-solvers* and greatly facilitated the implementation of her retreats.

Demand increased and the scope of the workshops widened as Elisabeth realized that within the very lessons she was learning from the dying was a prescription for life, lessons she felt compelled to share with as many people as possible. By getting in touch with their deepest and long-repressed pain, guilt, fear, and shame, participants were then taught that they could literally live until they died with a sense of acceptance, serenity, peace, and forgiveness. The intensive, week-long experience was geared toward helping people overcome the tears and anger in their lives. These emotionally challenging experiences could be the death of a parent never mourned, sexual abuse never admitted, or any other traumatic event or experience. By thus relinquishing their unfinished business, they would have released the negativity within them and would be more equipped to contend with whatever windstorms might befall them.

Before the purchase of Shanti Nilaya in 1977, the retreat center in Escondido, California, Kübler-Ross would hold her workshops with 40 to 60 participants at secluded hotels, retreat centers, even monasteries and convents, any place providing the basic criterion of privacy, both for the larger group and the individual participants. While there was no written schedule, all workshops followed the same basic format and were comprised of group lectures, interviews with dying patients, question and answer sessions, and one-to-one sessions. All participants would meet immediately after breakfast through the remainder of the day and evening, sometimes not breaking until the early hours of the morning. Everyone would sit on the circle, with those unable to sit on the floor in chairs outside the larger circle. Participants would have been asked to bring any musical instrument so that every day would begin with singing and music, a lesson Kübler-Ross had learned from Native Americans, Benedictine monks, and all religious services around the globe. The act of singing together increases a group's energy and is a true celebration of the human soul.

Appreciating my keen attention to her revolutionary concepts of living and dying, she smiled broadly and provided me with an invitation to living by saying, "Dick, I want you to come to my next workshop." I nodded my head, searching for a valid reason to avoid living. I harnessed all of my intellectual energy derived from my extensive academic experience and concocted what I thought was an indefensible reason why I could not attend her workshop and be alive. I explained, "Elisabeth, I would love to. But your retreat center is not accessible to persons with disabilities!" Realizing that I had confabulated an irrefutable excuse to remain emotionally dead, I further explained that I could not attend the conferences that are held on the second floor of the center. Smiling victoriously, she said, "I will immediately get you an elevator so you can attend my workshop." The debate ended with my realization that I had met my match. I said, "I look forward to being with you at your next retreat." She signed a copy of her book, *On Death and Dying*, with this short, seven-word sentence: "You have taken a long trip over the mountain. Love, Elisabeth."

As I returned home, I was very perplexed by the outcome of my visit. "I had risked my life driving on this torturous road, hoping to find out about dying and then signed up for a retreat on living!" Little did I know that it would take the entire five days of the workshop to understand fully that I would have to have the courage and honesty to look within myself to identify whatever prevented me from living passionately and expressing unconditional love. Only by reliving my pain, anguish, and sorrows could I be able to live more positively and more fully until my death and accept it without fear.

Because I busied myself with many of the mindless activities at the University, I was skilled enough to avoid thinking about my conversations with Elisabeth and the impending retreat. Prior to the appointed week, I collected "important" manuscripts and grant proposals that I would complete during my planned breaks throughout the retreat. I had made plans for the best of both worlds: a spiritual awakening and revolutionary surgical discoveries. As I returned on the tortuous road to Head Waters, I had thoughts of several innovations, suggestions that might

Dr. Elisabeth Kübler-Ross. Graphite illustration by Ned Bittinger.

improve her workshop. First, I thought that the retreat should be short-
ened to two days so as not to interfere with the work week. Second, I
thought it would be ideal to move the retreat closer to Charlottesville so
that the participants could enjoy Jefferson's academic village. Third, I
believed that the retreat should focus more on the process of dying rather
than living, which was what had led me to seek out Elisabeth in the first
place.

Upon arrival at the retreat, Elisabeth greeted me, pointing to the new
motorized elevator attached to the staircase. She exclaimed, "When you
ride in this elevator, you will feel like you are flying!" Thirty-nine other
individuals gathered for this retreat. When I introduced myself to the
other participants, I was very impressed by their level of motivation as
measured by the length of their respective journeys. Much to my surprise, I was the only person who lived within 100 miles of Head Waters.
Others had survived the tortuous roads of Virginia mountains as well as
jet travel from every continent. Participants from New York, Florida,
California, and Washington filled the American contingency. This international gathering of spiritual adventurers provided additional credibil-
ity to the potential value of the workshop. A dinner replete with
vegetables, fruits, and bread all made at the farm whetted our appetites
for the living journey. Elisabeth and six facilitators identified the lodgings
for each participant so they could enjoy a restful night.

The ring of a cowbell awakened us to a race for the bathrooms, after
which we would sit down to our first delicious breakfast with a wide
assortment of fresh fruit. While the participants walked up to the first
conference, I took my first air flight to the second floor with the assistance of one of the facilitators. After making a safe landing, I wheeled
into the conference room in which all participants sat in a circle. The
conference room had a large skylight allowing the sun to illuminate the
room. The green leaves of the trees outside leaned close to the windows
and moved gently in the mountain breezes. There were only two unusual
features of the conference room: eight mattresses piled in a corner and
heaps of Yellow Pages set beside them.

The conference began with wonderful music and featured the Irish
songstress, Phyllida Templeton, whose lullabies soothed us into believing
that this was a safe and loving environment. When the peaceful melodies
ended, the humanity of the retreat became readily apparent. Expecting
the facilitators to be teachers, I was shocked that they were human beings
who shared their own pain, anguish, agony, and anger and discussed how

they had the courage and honesty to look within themselves to relive their pain so that they could live their lives more positively and fully. They all thanked each of the participants for the honor of learning from them and having the participants as their teachers. Each facilitator assured us that this retreat was a safe environment in which confidentiality was a prerequisite. Furthermore, they encouraged all of us to express our emotions and assured us that comfort would be provided if a distressed participant requested it. Alcohol and drugs without a prescription would not be permitted. The facilitators' presentation was an invitation for each of us to present our life experiences and discuss our *goals* for the retreat. Each of us dealt with aspects about ourselves that prevented open communication, our own fears, anxieties, shame, guilt, negative memories and conditioning. Discussions revolved around issues of denial and "playing games." That afternoon, as well as the third and fourth days, the facilitators positioned the eight mattresses on the carpeted floor of the conference center. The participants were divided into groups of six with one facilitator for each group. Each group was then positioned around a mattress. One participant with a facilitator would sit on the mattress.

Within minutes, the conference center was transformed from a peaceful, spiritual setting into a room saturated with explosive, pent-up emotions of anger and fear, combined with tears flowing down our cheeks. As participants shared their hearts, they suddenly became the mirrors for our souls. It was easy for me to see my own pent-up rage, anger, and guilt, harbored deep in my soul. Tears flowed from my eyes as an acknowledgment of my soulmates' externalization of their own emotions. As a participant struck the mattress with a rubber hose, this action symbolized their rage and anger. Often the exhausted warrior would slip to the mattress, sobbing words of sadness that ultimately would transform into those of forgiveness. Their brave testimonies captured my attention to such a degree that time had no meaning until I was welcomed to the loving center stage of attention. Because my disability obviously interfered with the externalization of my anger about my profound physical and personal losses, I had to resort to yelling and screaming. Because I could not see any secondary gain from my disability, my rage was transformed into feelings of hopelessness, causing me to sob. When the facilitator positioned a pillow under my cheek, I felt a renewed contact with the human race that restored my hope in living. As my tears dried, I felt the hands of the six participants and the facilitator gently grasp my arms and legs, raising me toward the skylight. They became my arms and legs, which gave me new strength as well as new insight into looking at my illness. Cradled in their arms, they gently swayed me back and forth as if I was flying. All of us were in union at that moment, no boundaries, no differences, just the purity of touching and being touched. I had hoped this levitation would be endless, but my flight had to end with a peaceful landing on my wheelchair. My smile to each of them seemed to be sufficient acknowledgment of their gift to me. I no longer had to view my illness as a lonely journey, but one that could be joyful and loving, especially if I had the courage to ask for help.

Elisabeth called this process of venting our emotions the "active externalization of negativities." The mattresses and phone books were benign outlets for our anger. When one person after another spontaneously moved to the mattress and began banging away, they released their pent-up rage, fear, guilt, and pain. In this crying out of our emotions, we were releasing ourselves from being its captive. In this setting, each of us took off our masks and admitted that we, too, had pains, fears, guilt, and angers. The workshop became more than just a process of externalization and expulsion of negative emotions. The larger message was how to live as well as how to die. I learned that message only when we are not afraid to live, will we be unafraid to die. Elisabeth pointed out that healing does not occur only at an individual level. Because each individual is connected through a vast network of relationships to innumerable other people, the process of healing even one person has far-reaching ramifications. While each individual touched my heart, I was impressed by some of the common themes expressed at the workshop. Sexual abuse was a source of enormous grief, anger, and rage for many women. I was shocked by the identity of the abusers, particularly physicians and clergy held in such high esteem by society. When abused by these powerful individuals, it was especially frustrating to the women that their abusers were not punished by the legal system and continued to reap the rewards of their status. The cries of the African-American community reverberated through the walls of the conference center. The legacy of their ancestral slavery had obviously not been resolved within their lives as they contended daily with the tremendous obstacles presented by our current social system. I was also impressed by the fact that the terminally ill patients attending the conference appeared to be the most generous and honest participants, who gave unconditionally a loving, helping hand. Everyone agreed that they were the ultimate teachers.

Those participants with something too intimate or lengthy to share with the entire group would meet with facilitators in a smaller group, providing them the unhurried space to go to the depths of their pain. During these moments of sharing, boundaries between facilitators and participants would blur, as those sharing their pain instinctually reached to comfort one another.

On Thursday morning, Elisabeth shared her own experience with the group, described how being a triplet left her devoid of an individual identity and used this as an example of grace and blessing as it had helped her to understand others with similar problems. She completed the day by discussing her beliefs about our natural emotions and the quadrants that make up our total being. She encouraged us to evaluate the events of our lives and understand the so-called coincidences, or what she called divine manipulations. The group began to feel an incredible upsurge, feelings of love, compassion, and understanding never experienced or felt before. On the final day, the group felt an uncommon togetherness after sharing so much pain and releasing so much anguish. We began to settle down in a calm and open manner, reflecting on the reasons why we make life so miserable for ourselves when it was designed to be so simple and so full of miracles.

The night before the final day of the conference, the inner peace we felt had been symbolically grounded during the fire ritual, where we sat around an open fireplace. After sharing with the group why we believed we had come to the workshop and what we felt we had attained through the four days of intense growth work, each of us threw a pine cone into the fire, into which we symbolically placed all the negativity we had relinquished over the past four days. One by one, interrupted only by singing or the playing of instruments, we stepped forward and shared what aspects of our personality we were to let go. At the fire ritual, I appreciated one of the new secondary gains of my disability. Seated in my wheelchair, it was fortuitous that each participant walked by me, nearing the fireplace. I was the bene-factor of a hug from each of the participants. This emotional experience answered one of the most important questions in life regarding the number of hugs that one individual needs. The indisputable answer is never enough. This contact reacquainted me with the physicality and intimacy I had enjoyed prior to my illness. At that moment, I realized the power of touch and the freedom of allowing yourself to love and be loved. Finally, loaves of bread baked by some of the participants were shared with a glass of wine in another simple symbolic act of sharing and gratitude.

Telephone numbers and addresses were exchanged so that each of us felt safe in the knowledge that we would be able to reach out to someone, once having returned home.

It is very difficult to define in words the benefits of the workshop experiences because the experiences felt and shared are on an experiential, almost nonverbal level. It is the intensity of love, care, courage, and honesty of the participants in the workshops that is impressive and ultimately transforms their lives. While these workshops last only five days, they become a catalyst for growth that continues over months and years. I can assure you that patients with quadriplegia or paraplegia especially benefit from these meetings. These individuals are often treated as dependent, vulnerable human beings who have to be overprotected or shielded from any emotional reactions. Some have been badly neglected, causing them to build up tremendous shields around their feelings in order to appear stoic and insensitive. These workshops are a safe place for such individuals to share the anguish, agony, and pain about their physical losses. When other individuals without physical disabilities share the anguish of the disabled, they become their limbs, their hands, and their legs.

Appreciating my limited psychomotor skills in hugging, I enlisted the wisdom and skill of my wife to teach me the science of hugging after the workshop.[3] She reminded me that the most emotionally fulfilling hug was the hug of presence, which is comforting to both individuals. The hug of presence is accomplished by first encircling your arms around your loved one. Position one hand over your loved ones' upper back, with the other hand over the lower back; the distance between your hands is approximately 12 inches. Spread your fingers widely apart. Apply firm, but gentle pressure with your fingers, palms and forearms to your beloved's back. Because the hug of presence is an emotional experience, it lasts indefinitely continuing beyond the physical separation.

Elisabeth has pointed out that not all participants have had such profound positive experiences from the workshops. Those individuals with children who have committed suicide have considerable difficulty in resolving their enormous grief. A child's suicide is especially hard to accept when our own expectations to have our children gratify our needs makes the loss of such a child even more unbearable. As we begin to understand that we have to live out our own lives and that we have free choice to lay claim to our own emotions, we can then face life as a challenge, not a threat.

It was very difficult for me to leave this nurturing loving environment at Healing Waters Farm because it provided a renewed sense of hope and allowed me to celebrate the beauty of my soul, rather than mourn the weakness of my limbs. Excited by these life- transforming experiences, I thought it would be wonderful for the entire University of Virginia to attend one of Elisabeth's retreats. Realizing that it would be difficult to have all 20,000 members of the University attend, I negotiated a compromise that nurtured my soul, an annual lunch with Elisabeth at her retreat. This event was extremely popular, especially for the students who still were not too busy to be alive. As I reflect on these subsequent seminars, I must confess that I'm not sure whether Elisabeth's home-cooking or seminar was the highlight of the conference. In any event, Elisabeth was the master speaker who captured the hearts of all the students. She used several interesting techniques to engage the audience. Speaking with her Swiss accent, she would occasionally search for words that would clarify a particular point. Students would immediately come to her rescue, yelling out literally hundreds of helpful synonyms. After choosing the word that she liked, her smile to the gifted student would be an acknowledgment of this contribution to her life. Second, her speeches were filled with the "I" word as she freely shared stories about her own personal journeys. Even at the University of Virginia, students rarely hear teachers share their souls because they wear so much scholarship on their sleeves. Elisabeth's seminar would focus on two important teachings that must be integrated into our personal living transformation. In these lessons, she described to us natural emotions and the quadrants of the human being (Appendix A).

Nearing the end of her seminar, Elisabeth made some profound predictions about our world. It seems to her that the whole planet is a terminally ill patient at this time. Most people know that global levels of stress are building to a dangerous point, and the planet is threatened by environmental catastrophe. The conclusion is that there must inevitably be a global cleansing to eliminate the hatred, greed, pain, grief, and rage that have been repressed for so long. In other words, a process similar to the one that occurs in her workshops must happen to the planet as a whole if the Earth is to survive.

Elisabeth's teachings have transformed my daily existence. Her beautifully simple philosophy continues to be taught in workshops, now called Externalization Workshops, around the world by people who had staffed her retreat centers. These workshops are residential weekends where one can explore, in a safe, confidential and accepting setting, how our bottled up emotions prevent us from fully living and enjoying each day. It is an opportunity for self-discovery and for healing of wounds, old or new, that deplete our energy and enthusiasm for life, lead us to fatigue and burnout at work and hinder us from fully giving and receiving love and affection. The emphasis of the workshop is on **YOU**, an individual that often remains neglected, overlooked and unappreciated.

I would urge you to attend one of these workshops (Appendix B). Carpe diem!

9

Surgeon's Transformation

Because *goal setting* is an important step in managing a *life-defining experience*, I have tried to enumerate for you some of these *goals* at different phases of my life. When I was a practicing surgeon, one of my most important *goals* was to develop a model emergency medical system in the Commonwealth of Virginia that would save thousands of lives. In addition, I challenged the University of Virginia to construct a burn and wound healing center to care for seriously ill patients. Our research laboratory wanted to develop drugs and products to improve patient care with the assistance of innovative companies in a modern research park. After developing MS, I added new *goals* focusing on rehabilitation medicine and curing my illness. As I added additional *goals* to my life, I became a crisis manager trying to convert *problems into opportunities*. It was as if I was swimming against a pounding surf waiting for another huge wave to challenge me. I became a real burn surgeon, putting out the fires of life.

Fortunately, Elisabeth Kübler-Ross rescued me from crisis management, burnout and stress. She provided me with the lessons that allowed me to get off the roller coaster ride so that I could smell and enjoy the flowers of life. Her lessons became a wakeup call for living. Following her advice, I devised an emergency plan to resuscitate my soul.[1,2] I took a three-pronged approach that consisted of (1) participating in annual social events, (2) pursuing artistic enrichment, and (3) transforming my business travel into opportunities for secondary spiritual gains.

I have immersed my life in annual social events that I enjoy with dear colleagues and friends. The value of participating consistently in these life celebrations in our community has become an integral part of my personal transformation. I have been thrilled by the Virginia Film Festival of American Film at the University of Virginia, which is a unique and nationally significant cultural event featuring serious discussion and academic exchange about America's liveliest art. Its success has been attributed to its clear definition of its role as a study of American film. One of the most memorable festivals was the one in which the theme was "Film Noir: Through a Lens Darkly." The term *film noir* is used today to describe Hollywood films of the 1940s and 1950s. The smoke-filled films portrayed that dark and gloomy world of crime and corruption, films in which it is often hard to distinguish the hero from the villain. The films are both pessimistic, cynical, and disillusioned.

Robert Mitchum was the star attraction as one who embodied *film noir*. Mitchum, with those heavy-lidded eyes that have seen it all, epitomizes cool. During his career that has spanned half a century, he played a variety of characters- good guys, bad guys, sensitive guys- but whatever the role, each has been unmistakably stamped a Mitchum character.

Roger Ebert also led a three-part, six-hour workshop of a shot-by-shot analysis of one of the world's greatest films, Billy Wilder's "Sunset Boulevard" (1950). This workshop allowed me to broaden my understanding of the choices, techniques, and strategies used to create the expressive power of the film. I gave a Ebert a "thumbs-up" for his superb course.

Each fall, I now attend the Convocation held on the lawn of the University of Virginia. During this ceremony, intermediate honors are bestowed on undergraduate students who have a grade point average of 3.4 or better in their first four semesters. One of the highlights of recent years was speaker Rita Dove, Commonwealth Professor of English at the University. Rita had been installed as Poet Laureate of the United States, the youngest and first African American to be so honored. In 1987, Rita won the Pulitzer Prize for *Thomas and Beulah*,[3] a collection of short stories based on the lives of her maternal grandparents.

In her speech, she reminded us that poetry makes the inner life of an individual known to others. "Through poetry, we can express empathy, a communion of the souls." She also stressed the importance of multicultural education, citing an African proverb: "It takes an entire village to educate a child." Villages take many forms, from neighborhoods to global communities. Rita indicated that, "We will remain children in some of these villages, continuing to be educated while educating others." After each Convocation, I especially enjoy the reception when I meet the proud parents and congratulate the student scholars.

Her speech reminded me that students at the University of Virginia often miss one of the most important aspects of their educational experiences, a community of caring. I believe that the academic experience alone is not enough to prepare students for life after formal education. A community of caring is needed to ensure that each student feels loved and supported by fellow students and faculty. A community of caring is best achieved through a simple, age-old concept: mentoring. By truly being *present in the moment*, listening, advising and working together with their fellow students, they will gain skills that will benefit everyone with whom they come in contact. To facilitate a culture of caring at the University, I felt that a formal mentoring program should be established throughout the University. I enlisted the help of some powerful *problem-solvers*, Kim Henderson (Princeton, New Jersey), Dr. Paul Yoder (Harrisonburg, Virginia) and Joseph Scherpf (Wilton, Connecticut) to establish endowments for scholarships for students who excel in mentoring. In this new developing culture of caring, students are being acknowledged annually by their peers for their commitment and service to mankind.

My pursuit of artistic enrichment was a pleasant experience because it was a retreat to wonderful childhood memories. I have become a patron of the arts, following in the footsteps of my father. Like his father, my father is a physician in family medicine whose office is in New York City. He started his practice in Greenwich Village, a part of Manhattan that has an artistic-bohemian character. The Village has closely packed brownstones, narrow streets with illogical routes, and an enticing assortment of restaurants and taverns. The most unique feature of the Village is its writers, teachers, entertainers, and especially artists who dominate the scene. My father developed close personal friendships with a large number of artists, many of whom became his patients. His appreciation of a wide range of art made him a reliable patron of artists and collector of their work. They were frequent visitors to our home and became an extended family.

My warmest memories of this artistic community centered around Franz Kline, who considered himself to be an adopted New Yorker. Born in Wilkes-Barre, Pennsylvania, in 1910, Franz developed an interest in art during high school and planned to pursue a career in illustration and cartooning. He began training as an illustrator in Boston and continued his education in London, where he met his future wife, Elizabeth, a model in one of his drawing classes. Elizabeth had been a ballet dancer for several years before they met. After leaving London, Franz and his wife settled in a one-room, cold water flat in Greenwich Village.

While determined to make his art support his family, Franz often had
to resort to sign-painting, frame-making, and carpentry. Franz painted
the murals in the Bleeker Street Tavern and in El Chico's, a Spanish
restaurant, which enhanced his visibility in the artistic community. More
important to his survival were his two reliable patrons, my father and a
Long Island executive.

My father first commissioned Franz to paint portraits of my older
brother, Ted, and me. Franz had a rough-hewn face, Bentonesque mus-
tache, long brown hair parted down the middle of his forehead, and a
large gentle smile that made my brother and me feel very comfortable.
Franz seemed always accessible, patient, endlessly good-natured, and he
displayed a high level of tolerance for two boys, seven and eight years old.
He immediately won us over by asking us to pose for the portraits in our
favorite outfits. We abandoned our ties and sport jackets in favor of our
favorite sweaters with reindeer prints. Franz courageously survived our
wiggling, squirming, and wisecracks during those seemingly endless
sittings. When he completed our portraits, we tested his patience by
asking him to paint a picture of our one-year old brother, Stephen, who
was sleeping, sucking his thumb. Franz completed Stephen's picture on
a piece of cardboard. Inspired by this accomplishment, we asked him to
paint the emblems of our favorite football teams on two mugs, which he
graciously completed.

My relationship with Franz had another important dimension, an
introduction to my father's practice of medicine. I accompanied my
father on a house call to Franz's apartment, at which time I met his wife,
Elizabeth. Suffering from depression and schizophrenia, she was later
hospitalized in Central Islip State Hospital for six months. Sometime
later, she was readmitted for 12 years. My father's concern for Franz and
his wife as well as their gratitude for his care were powerful memories
that considerably influenced my decision to pursue a career in medicine.

Franz's visits to our home continued through my adolescence. He
made a painting of Washington Square in Greenwich Village on a folding
screen that my father placed in front of an examining table in his office.
He also commissioned Franz to paint a portrait of Mohandas Karam-
chand Ghandi, the preeminent leader of Indian nationalism and the
proponent for nonviolence of this century. Franz's paintings of Nijinsky
as Petrouchka and scenes of Greenwich Village and Lehigh Valley also
hung on the walls of our living room. One of my favorite paintings was
a self-portrait of our beloved Franz. On my walks to and from school, I

would see him entering or leaving Cedars Tavern, between 8th and 9th Streets on University Place and was always greeted by his warm wave and smile.

In the 1950s, Franz's painting turned away from his representational literal style and moved toward abstract expressionism. Using inexpensive commercial paints and large house painter's brushes, he painted graphic networks of bars of black paint on white backgrounds, creating positive shapes with the white areas within the black strokes. When I asked Franz about his shift in style and perspective, he explained that abstract expressionistic art is the inherent authenticity of personal expression, which is derived from the unconscious mind of painters who have a deeply personal and uncompromising commitment to the art of painting. He told me that the Cedars Tavern, the nondescript neighborhood bar where I so often saw him, was the artistic cathedral for our culture at that time, whose clientele became the leading edge of avant-garde and changed the direction of painting throughout the world. Although these artists did not form a stylistically cohesive group, they recognized with reservation the various labels that critics and, later, art historians placed on them: New York School, Action Painters, or most commonly, abstractionists. Most notable among them were Pollock, de Kooning, and Kline, who remained close friends. Jackson Pollock was the most discussed new artist in the United States, if not in the world. In 1947, Pollock began to paint his pictures by laying large canvases on the floor and pouring liquid paint directly from the can, often with the aid of a dip stick. During the same time, William de Kooning, a Dutch-born American painter, was developing his own style that led to the fusion of his figurative and abstract modes of painting. He was remarkably personal in his touch, leaving drips and accidents as signs of his spontaneous action on the canvas.

Inspired by our family's relationship with Franz, I have renewed my interest in being a patron of the arts. Because Virginia is blessed with so many notable resident artists, it was easy to identify two individuals, Fred Nichols and Ned Bittinger, whose work I especially enjoy. I particularly appreciated Fred's work, whose watercolor paintings have become a living memory for me as well as my loved ones. Since coming to Virginia, I have been especially fascinated by its picturesque lakes. During each Fall, the colorful leaves provide a magical kaleidoscope filled with wonderful memories. I asked Fred to paint a scene from Lake Sherando that is nestled in the Blue Ridge Mountains. The next watercolor I commissioned celebrated the beauty of Mirror Lake, next to our home, that is now surrounded by large evergreens that my wife, Carol, planted. I have given prints of both of these watercolors to my beloved children, my "adopted" children, colleagues in this community and friends throughout the world, serving as living memories of our deep, everlasting friendships. I hope that these beautiful prints serve as constant reminders of my love and respect for these extraordinary people.

Fred Nichols' body of work serves as an ambassador for the beautiful state of Virginia to the rest of the world. His skill as a formally trained artist coupled by his bright, celebratory interpretations of our natural world create loving portraits of places we are sometimes too busy to appreciate fully. Having grown up in Charlottesville, son of a University of Virginia professor of architectural history, Fred had always been encouraged by his family to pursue his early interest in creating art. He was fortunate to find his first true patron when his third grade teacher encouraged him to paint during recess, while other children romped in the playground. Fred transformed their classroom into his first gallery. "From that point on, I knew I wanted to be an artist," he says.

Fred pursued a formal artistic education at the University, one of only three art majors in the late 1960s. He concentrated on painting scenes from the local area and began to formulate his philosophy. "The objective of my art is to recreate the natural world that surrounds and forms us. We are increasingly separate from nature, living more and more in a man-made and designed environment. Through my study of the wilderness, I hope to renew interest and desire – not only to protect but appreciate the natural world." It comes as no surprise that Fred felt a lack of inspiration when he moved to New York City to attend the Pratt Art Institute. Buildings and people constantly intruded on his subjects. So, this Southern immigrant would return, armed with a camera, to his homeland in central Virginia, where he would photograph innumerable settings. He would take these back to Pratt and use them as guides, or "templates" as he calls them, for his paintings.

For more than 20 years, Fred has continued this process, hiking around the Virginia wilderness, taking photographs, then recreating them in his own unique style. After converting the photo to a slide, he then projects it onto a canvas. "Like a jigsaw puzzle, I take the photograph apart and put it back together as a painting." The projected slide becomes a window through which Fred continues to experience the subject of his painting without leaving his studio. The end result is Fred's impressionistic view of this snapshot, filled with a surprising color palette and a vibrancy that celebrates these "moments" in nature. When I look at Fred's paintings, I am reminded of the necessity to simply stop sometimes, and look around at the natural wonders that surround us.

I started another artistic adventure with Ned Bittinger who is recognized for his wide range of artistic accomplishments. He is one of the premier portrait artists in the country and has painted renowned political leaders, statesmen, and educators. Among his most celebrated clients are Secretary of State James Baker and actress Shirley MacLaine. Seven of his portraits grace the halls of the University of Virginia. Bank presidents, judges, and corporate leaders are his stock in trade. During the last few years, his illustrious career has expanded into a new field, the illustration of children's books. His latest endeavor, *A Rocking Horse Christmas*, has been acclaimed by American Book Sellers as their "pick of the list" and all indications point to this first effort as a resounding success.[4] For Ned, this new direction has opened a whole new world of possibilities. Now, instead of catering to the desires of one client at a time, he can imagine a world and paint with more freedom to choose perspective, color, and mood. Reading *A Rocking Horse Christmas* is a lush adventure, the fanciful illustrations vastly appealing to children and adults alike. This combination of imagination and skilled portrait artistry made him the ideal candidate to paint the cover for this book. Moreover, his graphic illustration within the chapters provides a powerful dimension to the exciting adventures in my life.

My latest adventure as a patron of the arts was with my best friend and wife, Carol Taylor, who is a magical theatrical performer. Carol starred as Maria in Leonard Bernstein's Broadway musical, *West Side Story*, which is considered by many to be one of the finest and most original works in the musical theatre. Carol is an electrifying performer who enchants the audience. Because Carol has been a loyal partner in all of my quests, I asked her if she could put my book, *Profiles for Success*, to music in a CD that would be a companion to my written adventures. In her CD, *From Somewhere in My Heart*, she sings enthralling, exquisite music from some of the most exciting musical plays, including *West Side Story* and *Man of La Mancha*, the latter being an adaptation of *Don Quixote*. From this unbiased critic, I judge her performance with the most extravagant adjectives: superb, imaginative, compelling, witty, inspirational and moving. A triumph!

Finally, my business travel immediately changed into a search for opportunities to expand my spiritual horizons. Together with friends, I

Prescription for Living

We must embrace our natural emotions as our friends.

Our natural emotions allow us to live our lives to the fullest, to experience the many joys of being human. If we foster and encourage in ourselves and in our children *natural* manifestations of fear, jealousy, grief, anger, and love, we will all reach a physical, emotional, intellectual, and spiritual harmony. The end result is inner peace.

We must have the courage and honesty to look within ourselves, to identify whatever prevents us from using our natural emotions positively.

We will recognize that fear and guilt are our only enemies. We must find a safe place where we can get in touch with our negativity, relive our pain, our anguish, our agony and anger, so that we may emerge free and purified and able to live more positively and more fully.

We must take ownership of our own emotions.

Most people *react to* rather than *act in* life; their awareness of the present is clouded by regrets in the past and fear of the future. We must take responsibility for all our choices, deeds, words, and thoughts. By thus being *present in the moment*, we will have no regrets and be equipped with the tools necessary to forge our own destinies.

We must touch and be touched through sharing.

Nothing is unspeakable. We give someone a gift when we share our pain. While they naturally cannot feel ours, hearing of it touches upon their own pool of pain, enabling them to share their own. It is our choice whether we want to continue living as silent victims of resentment, negativity, the need for revenge; or whether we elect to vocalize, leave the negativity behind, and view our tragedies as the windstorms of life that can both strengthen us and help us grow.

We must face life as a challenge, not as a threat.

Life is dominated by randomness. It is up to us to be open to understanding its significance. There is purpose and meaning in everything that happens to us and around us, as long as we are there, *present in the moment*, to learn our lesson. In our most anguished moments may reside the greatest of gifts.

The ultimate lesson we must learn is how to love and be loved unconditionally.

We must learn to understand rather than to judge, to give and receive, and to love without expectation of reward. Actions taken with the intent of helping others will, in the end, always work out. Even mistakes made with honesty, purity, and love can produce positive outcomes.

We must do only what we love to do.

Who we are is a culmination of the choices we have made. We may have fewer material things: less money, a smaller house, a cheaper car. But we will totally live. If we tap into the true passion of what we love, the rest will follow. Each day is another line on our epitaph and we must live and write the story as the legacy we wish to leave behind.

We must embrace the opportunity for experiential seminars and group interactions.

There is an unexplained transformation, power, and wisdom that occur in the presence of authentic sharing. This process, however simple as it sounds, is only rarely experienced by many people.

One important lesson Elisabeth learned from the dying patient was that during the process of facing death, we have unique opportunities to reexamine and reorder our lives so that we can love people unconditionally. If people could express this naturally, there would be eternal peace. This harmony has obviously not yet been achieved because, in part, there is a conspiracy of silence within our society surrounding our sometimes brutal and inhumane history.

now planned a recreational event during each scientific meeting that nurtured my soul. At the beginning of this transformation, I did experience some hesitancy, which was derived from the mistaken belief that hard-working physicians should not make time for fun, and that play is incompatible with learning by serious academic scholars. For those of you who may have similar misgivings, I hope that this story will help you overcome your anxiety and inhibition toward personal enjoyment.

My first spiritual journey began at a scientific meeting in Toronto. I decided that I would complement this superb academic meeting with an adventure to a Toronto Bluejays baseball game. I discovered that securing tickets to this event was a major undertaking. Attempts to call the stadium led to numerous busy signals as the operator answered continued requests for seats. When I finally reached the ticket office, they applauded my efforts by saying that I had purchased the last two seats in the 52,000-seat stadium. With this realization, I knew that I had achieved a major spiritual victory. My recreational venture to the SkyDome was a memorable event. From the outside, the SkyDome looked like an oversized starship. People were streaming toward it, and the air was saturated with the collective murmur that is heard before any big sporting event. Once inside, I was seated near the first base line. Two features of the SkyDome immediately caught my attention. The roof, which opened 674 feet, was closing to maintain a comfortable temperature within the stadium. Its multiwheel drive mechanism, powered by what is known as "bogies," closed the roof within 30 minutes. Jumbotron, the world's largest television, loomed in the Dome's center with Orwellian omniscience. Jumbotron displayed stats, scores, instant replays, team information, and brilliant computer images, all on a screen that measured 110 feet by 33 feet. Jumbotron contained a full production facility with a five-camera input with a crew of 11 to 18. More than 43 prewired camera positions existed within the SkyDome to feed the camera inputs.

My trip back to the hotel provided another noteworthy lesson. The lobby of the hotel was filled with many of my colleagues who were discussing their planned professional and recreational activities during this scientific meeting. They all showed considerable interest in going to the SkyDome. On contacting the concierge, they were told that the entertainment center was already sold out. I believed that they received this news with mixed feelings. On one hand, they were genuinely disappointed that they did not have the opportunity to see the SkyDome.

However, I perceived a sense of relief that they would not be tempted to enjoy themselves during the meeting.

This decision to see a baseball game during this scientific meeting was a premeditated plan to resuscitate my soul. This nurturing experience is now a catalyst for carefully planning each scientific meeting so that I have the unrivaled privilege of enjoying new recreational activities, such as opera, museums and Broadway shows. Failure to carefully plan for each meeting would usually result in a meeting devoid of empowering spiritual experiences because seats at these events will be "souled out."

Elisabeth Kübler-Ross has taught me how to embrace the gifts of life. I am now able to be *present in the moment* and enjoy the spiritual beauty in my family and friends. Since meeting Elisabeth and experiencing such a profound change in my perceptions of living, I have felt compelled to share these *profiles for success* in living. The following prescription is a distillation of her beautifully simple philosophy. I know it will resonate with you as it did with me.

10

Epilogue

What lessons have we learned from these seven gifted individuals who have transformed our society? First, each individual had a *life-defining experience* that caused him or her to establish well-defined *goals*. Let us review their *goals* and see how they transformed our world.

Dr. Owen Wangensteen watched most patients with acute intestinal obstruction die of operative surgery. Deeply saddened by the deaths of his beloved patients, he worked tirelessly to improve the management of intestinal obstruction. Dr. Wangensteen devised a nonoperative conservative management of intestinal obstruction that saved thousands of lives. His important scientific discovery showed all of his students that revolutionary advances in research could be achieved by multidisciplinary teams of scientists and surgeons. Surgeons working in his academic village in Minnesota became exciting surgical pioneers who developed open heart surgery, cardiac pacemakers, cardiac transplantation, pancreatic transplantation and the field of metabolic surgery for treatment of elevated blood cholesterol.

Their extensive military experiences convinced Drs. Jim Mills and R Adams Cowley that seriously injured patients could be saved by a well-organized military emergency medicine system. When Dr. Mills saw seriously ill patients treated in his hospital by inexperienced physicians, his *goal* became the training and certification of emergency physicians prepared to save the lives of the sick and injured. Dr. Cowley's *goal* was to save the lives of injured Americans. He devised a model trauma treatment center that has now been replicated throughout the world. Realizing the reluctance of civilian physicians to work in a coordinated emergency medical system, Dr. David Boyd's *goal* was to devise a coordinated and effective emergency medical system in our country. Dr.

Boyd's guidelines for coordinated emergency care have now been implemented in every state in our country.

Michaela and Augusto Odone courageously faced the devastating inherited demyelinating disease of their beloved son, Lorenzo, believing that they could achieve their *goal* of curing their son. Without medical credentials, both worked tirelessly to devise the first therapeutic treatment of their son's illness, adrenoleukodystrophy. Because Lorenzo did not gain many of the benefits of their revolutionary discovery, he now has permanent neurologic disability that they are trying to correct with new gene and drug therapies devised by their new comprehensive research program.

When pastoral students invited Elisabeth Kübler-Ross to join them in understanding death and dying, their talks with the dying patients became her *life-defining experience.* Her conversations with dying patients provided an understanding of the patients' emotional responses to dying as well as unexpected insights into the secrets of living. Her writing, lectures and seminars rescued the dying from isolation from society, allowing them to be cared for in loving hospices. Lessons about living learned from the dying patients became integrated into her workshop curriculum that allows participants to live a self-actualized life.

These courageous individuals redefined the perceptions of our lives and gave us the tools to reach for the stars. Their *Profiles for Success* for teaching, healing, curing, and living have several common themes that teach us about living a self-actualized life.

- You are born as a gifted, talented person who has unconditional love for people and this planet.
- You must be *present in the moment* and be fully aware of all that is around you. You must be able to hear the human suffering and pain of the afflicted.
- You are a talented and unique individual who can turn *obstacles into opportunities.*
- You can only accomplish changes in society if you have a *clear understanding of your goals.*
- You must enlist the help of other *powerful problem-solvers* who will clarify and define your *goals* as well as identify strategies for *societal transformation.*
- You will be faced with many convincing arguments that will encourage you to abandon your dream. Confused by your inability to

separate the message from the messenger, you will focus more on perceived personal limitations and inadequacies, causing you to give up the quest.

- The worst death in life is not death, but an emotional death during life.

The lessons learned from these teachers have transformed my life.

I have modeled my research program after that of Dr. Wangensteen, enrolling the help of a multidisciplinary team of scientists. Our investigations have resulted in the development of many drugs and products that allow wounds to heal without infection and adhesion formation. Burn patients, as well as those with complex wounds, are cared for in our new modern 16-bed burn and wound healing center. Our research team has been instrumental in starting an industrial research park that will bring further scientific advances to the patient's bedside. An endowed Chair for a basic scientist in our Plastic Surgery Department has been established to ensure that research will always be an integral part of this Department.

Lessons learned from Drs. Mills, Cowley and Boyd have allowed me to champion the development of a model emergency medical system in the Commonwealth of Virginia that has saved thousands of lives. The University of Virginia Health Sciences Center has implemented innovative advances in emergency medical care. A Department of Emergency Medicine has been established with a residency training program in emergency medicine. A trauma service, led by a skilled trauma surgeon, now directs the coordinated care of the trauma patient. An air evacuation system has been established to transport the seriously ill and injured patient safely back to the hospital. Special services have been added to our Emergency Department that include a computerized poison control system, behavioral crisis center, sexual assault resource center, and a life support learning center for educating health professionals. A modern telecommunications system allows the 18 different well-trained rescue squads to communicate with the radio communication centers in the Emergency Department. The public gains access to emergency care by a 911 communication system that is accessible to teletypewriters for the deaf.

The Odones have taught me that hope springs eternal and incurable diseases are curable. My development of MS was a *life-defining experience* that dramatically redefined my professional *goals* and caused me to develop a modern rehabilitation program for patients with MS and cure my illness. With the assistance of a multidisciplinary team of scientists, we devised an innovative aquatic therapy program for rehabilitation of patients with MS that is being used throughout the world. My interests in rehabilitation medicine had other beneficial effects on persons with disabilities at our hospital. I championed a $3-million renovation program that made our hospital accessible to persons with disabilities. In addition, a modern Department of Rehabilitation Medicine was established at the University of Virginia School of Medicine with a residency training program for physiatrists, physicians who specialize in rehabilitation medicine. With the help of my beloved friends, Charles and Beth Ross, we began our search to cure MS. Because one form of MS is caused by a retrovirus, a research team has been established to search for the cause and cure of this form of MS. An international symposium was held in September 1998 in Charlottesville, Virginia, that allowed world-renowned scientists to devise a plan to cure this retroviral infection that is being carried by an estimated 25 million people. A responsible, focused team of scientists must be identified that will quickly find the cure of this disease. A budget of $250 million is needed to achieve this result. Successful treatment of this neurologic disease has other obvious important implications. If well-funded, focused research can cure this chronic illness, one can conclude that similar courageous scientific programs can cure all chronic diseases, like cancer, heart disease, diabetes mellitus, Parkinson's disease, and even aging.

Elisabeth Kübler-Ross provided a wakeup call for my life that allows me to be *present in the moment* to the beauties of people who are the flowers of our planet. I am resuscitating my soul by being a patron of the arts and a champion for mentoring students. My love for the arts is best expressed in the new CD, *From Somewhere in My Heart*, recorded by my wife, Carol Taylor, who starred on Broadway as Maria in Leonard Bernstein's classic, *West Side Story*. I am also promoting a new culture of caring at the University of Virginia in a new student mentoring program. A special endowment has been established for scholarships for undergraduate and medical students who display exemplary service to their fellow students as mentors.

Life is good. I give this book as a gift to you as an emotional wakeup call for your life. One of my purposes in writing this book is to begin a dialogue between you and me. I welcome you to contact me by email at **profiles@cstone.net**, allowing you to share your dreams and to become my teacher. After reading this book, you may have a renewed perception of the meaning of your life. When you realize that life is incredibly precious, you will reorder your priorities. You will begin to appreciate the uniqueness and beauty that you alone possess, and celebrate and acknowledge these qualities in others. When you face loss or illness, it can be the beginning of a journey of self-exploration that focuses on unconditional love. This self-exploration will change the direction of your professional career, allowing you to contribute to society in a new and powerful way. How often the case has been that success has not been in spite of a loss or handicap, but because of it.

I can attest both as a physician and as a patient about the challenges of illness. Anything that evolves from a personal loss experience is not a function of the characteristic of loss, but of human nature. People have the natural capacity to affirm, acknowledge and embrace life in the most difficult of circumstances, and to help each other despite any obstacle. The reality is that healing happens between human beings. The wound in me inspires the healer in you; the wound in you invokes the healer in me, and then the two healers bond. Caring is inseparable from understanding, and like understanding, it must be inclusive. When you listen to someone, you hear yourself. When you care for another, you care for yourself. Healing occurs when you let another human being know that their suffering and fear matters to you.

e.e. cummings was an American poet and painter who first attracted attention in the age of literary experimentation with his eccentric punctuation and phrasing.[1] He took his iconoclastic view of life so seriously that he legally changed the spelling of his name to lower-case letters. His beautiful poetry and live lyrics have a childlike candor and freshness, which celebrate the beauty of our lives.

I thank You God for this most amazing
Day: for the leaping greenly spirits of trees
And a blue true dream of sky; and for everything
Which is natural which is infinite which is yes

(I who have died am alive again today,
and this is the sun's birthday and this is the birth
day of life and of love and wings: and of the gay
great happenings illimitably earth)

how should lasting touching hearing seeing
breathing any – lifted from me no

of all nothing – human merely being
doubt unimaginable You?
(now the ears of my ears awake and
now the eyes of my eyes are opened)

I wish for all of you a spiritual rebirth, allowing you to say, "I who have died am alive again today."

A Student's Perspective

each time in a new way
R. F. Edlich

You see beyond our,
seeming

Giving,
when some saw no offering

Transcending ominous tales
transcribed in denuding cells.

Leaving most too weak
steady do you keep
moving,
each time in a new way.

In your rising example I
strive,
hoping to find a glimpse,
of myself.

freeman suber
fourth year medical student
University of Virginia

Notes

Chapter1: My Invitation

1. Kübler-Ross E. *On Death and Dying*, Simon & Schuster, New York, NY, 1969.
2. de Unamuno y Jugo M. *The Life of Don Quixote and Sancho According to Miguel de Cervantes de Saavedra*, translated by Homer P. Earle, Albert A. Knopf, New York, NY, 1927.

Chapter 2: Teachers' Mission

1. Peltier LP, Aust JB. *L'Étoile du Nord An Account of Owen Harding Wangensteen (1898–1981)*, American College of Surgeons, Chicago, IL, 1994.
2. Edlich RF. Reflections on Wangensteen's academic village. *Am J Surg* 1981; 141: 601-604.
3. Edlich RF. What you need is a doctor. *J Emerg Med* 1989; 7: 665–669.
4. Sanes S. *A Physician Faces Cancer in Himself*, State University of New York Press, Albany, NY, 1979.
5. Henley WE. *A Book of Verses*, D. Nutt Press, London, 1881.
6. Lowell JR. *Under the Willows and other Works*, Fields Osgood Press, Boston, MA, 1868.
7. Edlich RF, Drescher EL. The princes and princesses of possibilities. *J Emerg Med* 1997;15: 101–105.

Chapter 3: Students' Journey

1. Edlich RF, Woods JA, Cox MJ. *Medicine's Deadly Dust: A Surgeon's Wake-up Call to Society*, Vandamere Press, Arlington, Virginia, 1997.
2. Lee CM, Lehman EP. Experiments with nonirritating glove powder. *Surg Gynecol Obstet* 1947;84:689–695.
3. Beezhold D, Beck WC. Surgical glove powders bind latex antigens. *Arch Surg* 1992; 127:1354–1357.

4. Edlich RF. The biology of wound repair and infection: a personal odyssey. *Ann Emerg Med* 1985; 14: 1018-1025.

5. Bryant CA, Rodeheaver GT, Reem EM, Nichter LS, Kenney JG, Edlich RF. Search for a nontoxic surgical scrub solution for periorbital lacerations. *Ann Emer Med*; 13:317-321.

6. Rodeheaver GT, Pettry D, Thacker JG, Edgerton MT, Edlich RF. Wound cleansing by high pressure irrigation. *Surg Gynecol Obstet* 1975; 141: 357-362.

7. Stevenson TR, Thacker JG, Rodeheaver GT, Bacchetta C, Edgerton MT, Edlich RF. Cleansing the traumatic wound by high pressure syringe irrigation. *J Am Coll Emerg Phys* 1976; 5: 17-21.

8. Herold DA, Rodeheaver GT, Bellamy WT, Fitton LA, Bruns DE, Edlich RF. Toxicity of topical polyethylene glycol. *Tox Appl Pharm* 1982; 65: 329-335.

9. Faulkner DM, Sutton ST, Hesford JD, Faulkner BC, Major DA, Hellewell TB, Laughon MM, Rodeheaver GT, Edlich RF. A new stable pluronic F-68 gel carrier for antibiotics in contaminated wound treatment. *Am J Emerg Med* 1997; 15: 20-24.

10. Gear AJL, Hellewell TB, Wright HR, Mazzarese PM, Arnold PB, Rodeheaver GT, Edlich RF. A new silver sulfadiazine water-soluble gel. *Burns* 1997; 23: 387-391.

11. Edlich RF, Attinger EO, Anné A, Ruffin W Jr., Haynes BW. Epidemiology and treatment of burn injury in Virginia. *J Burn Care and Rehab* 1984; 5: 275-281.

12. Miller A. The Drama of the Gifted Child. The Search for the True Self. Harper Collins Publishers, 1981.

Chapter 4: Healer's Adventure

1. Edlich RF. Three giant steps toward the development of modern emergency medical service system. *J Emerg Med* 1991; 9: 61-66.

2. Mills JD. A method of staffing a community hospital emergency department. *Va Med* 1963; 90: 518-519.

3. Franklin J, Doelp A. Shocktrauma, St. Martin's Press, New York, NY, 1980.

4. Boyd DR, Edlich RF, Micik S. *Systems Approach Emergency Medical Care*, Prentice-Hall, Norwalk, CT, 1983.

Chapter 5: Disciple's Expedition

1. Talbert S, White SD, Bowen JD, Stephens LM, Mapstone SJ, Spisson KR, Edlich RF. Improving emergency care of the sexual assault victim. *Ann Emerg Med* 1980; 9: 293-297.

2. Edlich RF, Clapp AR. Evolution of emergency services in central Virginia. *Virg Med* 1985; 112: 185-187.
3. Ricks TD, Whitehead WN, Stone D, Attinger EO, Edlich RF. Nine-one-one. *Virg Med* 1976; 103: 268–269.
4. Rockwell DD, Crampton RS, Mapstone SJ, Grant JE, Edlich RF, Garvin JM, Miller KP. New in Virginia: the shock-trauma emergency technician. *Virg Med* 1981; 108: 410–413.
5. Edlich RF. Virginia's trauma centers. *Virg Med* 1984; 111: 106-107.
6. Compton MV, Lattin-Souder M, Walsh WM III, Sanders E, Stier D, Spyker DA, Edlich RF. Computer-aided emergency telecommunications for the deaf. *Ann Emerg Med* 1982; 11: 324–326.
7. Boyd DR, Edlich RF, Micik S. *Systems Approach Emergency Medical Care*, Prentice-Hall, Norwalk, CT, 1983.

Chapter 6: Patient's Voyage

1. *Lorenzo's Oil*. Miramax Films; 1992.
2. Odone A, Odone M. Lorenzo's oil. A new treatment for adrenoleukodystrophy. *J Pediatr Neurosci* 1989; 5: 55–61.
3. Moser HW. Adrenoleukodystrophy: natural history, treatment, and outcome. *J Inher Metab Dis* 1995; 18: 435–447.
4. Naifeh SW, Smith GW. *Best Lawyers in America*, Woodward-White, Inc., Aken, SC, 1998.
5. Naifeh SW, Smith GW. *Best Doctors in America*, Woodward-White, Inc., Aken, SC, 1998.

Chapter 7: Physician-as-Patient's Quest

1. Harbison JW, Calabrese VP, Edlich RF. A fatal case of sun exposure in a multiple sclerosis patient. *J Emer Med* 1989; 7:465–467.
2. Israel DJ, Heydon KM, Edlich RF, Pozos RS, Wittmers LE. Core temperature response to immersed bicycle ergometer at water temperatures of 21°, 25°, and 29°C. *J Burn Care Rehab* 1989; 10: 336–345.
3. Zura RD, Groschel DHM, Becker DG, Hwang JC-S, Edlich RF. Is there a need for state health department sanitary codes for public hydrotherapy and swimming pools? *J Burn Care Rehab* 1990; 11: 146–150.
4. Tanner RW, Zura RD, Chen VT, Gregory PC, Becker DG, Thacker JG, Edlich RF. A system for adaptive transportation. *J Burn Care Rehab* 1990; 11: 543–551.
5. deHoll JD, Williams LA, Steers WD, Rodeheaver GT, Clark MM, Edlich RF. Technical considerations in the use of external condom catheter systems. *J Burn Care Rehab* 1992; 13: 664–672.

6. Walk EE, Ahn HC, Lampkin PM, Nabizadeh SA, Edlich RF. Americans with Disabilities Act. *J Burn Care Rehab* 1993; 14: 92–98.
7. Edlich RF, Neal JG, Suber F, Kirby D, Woods JA, Bentram D, McGowan J. A new barrier-free burn center. *J Burn Care Rehabil* 1998; 19: 390–398.
8. Bentrem DJ, McGovern EE, Hammerskjold M-L, Edlich RF. Human T-cell lymphotropic virus type-I (HTLV-I) retrovirus and human disease. *J Emerg Med* 1994; 12: 825–832.
9. De Thé G, Bomford R. An HTLV-I vaccine: why, how, for whom? *AIDS Research and Human Retroviruses.* 1993; 9:381–6.
10. Franchini G. An HTLV-I/II vaccine: from animal models to clinical trials. *Blood* 1995; 86: 3619–3639.
11. Aggarwal M, Manson TT, Edlich RF. Charities: a solution or a problem? *J Emerg Med* 1995; 13: 389–392.

Chapter 8: Lover's Search

1. Kübler-Ross E. *On Death and Dying*, Simon & Schuster, New York, NY, 1969.
2. Kübler-Ross E. *Working it Through*, Macmillan, New York, NY, 1982.
3. Edlich RF. Resolutions for graduating medical students: a pathway to self-transformations. *J Emerg Med* 1992:10: 747–752.

Chapter 9: Surgeon's Transformation

1. Edlich RF. Physician transformation from hero to lover. *Acad Emerg Med* 1995; 2: 845–847.
2. Edlich RF. Another life saved. *J Emerg Med* 1995; 13: 91–93.
3. Dove R. Selected Poems. Random House, New York, N.Y., 1993
4. Osborne MP, Bittinger N. *Rocking Horse Christmas*, Scholastic Press, New York, NY, 1997.

Epilogue

1. cummings ee. *Complete poems, 1904–1962*, WW Norton, New York, NY, 1991.

Elisabeth Kübler-Ross' Reflections

Natural Emotions

Elisabeth described the purpose of feelings, which she referred to as natural and unnatural (or distorted) emotions. For some it can be shocking and wonderful to discover that feelings have purposes as we are so often taught that feelings can be often inconvenient and "get in the way." Elisabeth contended, however, that we have these five natural emotions (fear, anger, jealousy, grief and love) so that we may be equipped to fulfill our destinies, experience life to its fullest potential, and have all the positive experiences that the physical life can offer a human being. Feeling, she told us, is how we know we are alive and how we respond to what life presents.

Unfortunately, she continued, the vast majority of us have been raised under the misconception that emotions are not our friends, that they must be repressed. Thus, they are replaced by unhealthy, unnatural, self-destructive emotions that wreak havoc on our personal lives and interpersonal relationships as they either explode or leak into the present. But, Elisabeth told us that if we have the strength and courage to confront our own emotions and to accept them as a part of us, not only could we take care of that unfinished business, but we could lead happier, healthier, even longer lives. Unexpressed emotions play out over long periods of time, draining us of valuable energy, whereas the natural manifestation of emotion expresses itself over a much shorter time, in the present. She pointed out that these distortions should not be qualified as "bad". After all, sometimes they are the best that we can do, especially when we're young. But Elisabeth's inherent message was that we don't have to live with them. We can express them as natural feelings. She told us to be gentle with ourselves as we learned to move away from distortions toward our natural feelings, learning to use them in their purposeful way.

She further emphasized that grief exists as a natural emotion to help us to deal with our losses which could be death, moving, losing a job, or the transition from one relationship to another. The natural expressions of grief are tears, the physiological response, and usually a compulsion to share one's grief. Elisabeth referred to the "thousand little deaths" we experience throughout our lives. She described examples of these little deaths — a gardener's loss of a favorite tree to drought or a child losing a favorite blanket. She pointed out that if loss has not been dealt with in an adequately healthy manner, our grief becomes distorted and we feel self-pity, we feel victimized, we feel misunderstood, and we spend our lives looking for others to fulfill our needs, which can never be gratified. Individuals holding onto unexpressed grief will live in the past, hide from the present, and be fearful of the future. If we allow ourselves to deal with those little deaths by naturally expressing our grief, by crying and sharing with others, we are then able to move on to the new challenges in life, unfettered by the negativity and turmoil of unexpressed grief.

She continued by describing the fundamental purpose of anger, another natural emotion. She told us that the natural purpose of anger is to initiate change. If you express anger in a relationship, it means something has shifted, something has changed. It also fuels a sense of assertiveness, allowing you to make a stand. Anger gives you the energy to draw the line and say "no." Elisabeth told us that natural anger only takes 15 seconds to express — an optimistic rate for most of us, but her point was well received. A person who has gotten in touch with their pooled natural anger can express it without storing it, can react and respond to it in a short amount of time — maybe a few minutes. By the time a two year old child having a temper tantrum finishes crying, she explained that he has gone all the way through the feeling and come out of it feeling refreshed, more than ready for the next obstacle. Elisabeth stressed that natural anger is a positive emotion because it causes harm to no one if the anger is dealt with compassionately and with understanding. If we are told as children that we can't say "no", if we are punished for being assertive and exerting our own inner authority, the inevitable pool of unexpressed anger distorts into hate and rage. Unexpressed hate will be internalized and turn against our bodies, more so than any other emotion. It will cause us to lash out at others, many times in sudden, explosive ways. Retaliation, the need for revenge, is also a distortion of anger and a manifestation that requires a tremendous amount of energy. Finally, those who have been taught to pool their anger will experience feelings of powerlessness, which can quickly translate into rage and contribute to physical sickness.

Elisabeth told us that while many of us may perceive jealousy as an infantile, "junior-high" emotion, it plays a critical and positive role in our development. It helps us to identify what we want, provides a stimulus to identify what may be missing from our lives, and things we would have liked to have or do. Jealousy can be very useful to help us to identify what we want and in what directions we wish to grow. Natural jealousy also promotes curiosity. But if this kind of natural jealousy is discouraged or belittled when we are children, we become judgmental, envious, hyper-competitive, and self-deprecating. We lose our self-esteem as we constantly compare ourselves to others and invariably come up short.

Elisabeth told us that we are born with only two natural fears, that of loud noises and falling. Every other fear is learned, she contended, passed onto children by adults as a projection of their own fears, insecurities, ambivalence, even hate and anger. One can easily add that there are other positive fears, like the hand that clutches your heart when you realize you are driving 20 miles over the speed limit on an icy road. Elisabeth's point was clear, however — if a fear serves no purpose, it can and should be relinquished. The natural purpose of fear is caution, a warning to slow down, to take it easy. Our natural fear keeps us healthy. But children who are raised to be afraid of the dark, afraid of other people, afraid of crossing the street, afraid to dare or risk, will not develop self-esteem and self-love. People with hidden, accumulated fear will be emotionally crippled, forever dependent on others and unable to gratify their own needs. They will be panicky, anxious, and prone to obsessive behavior.

Love's purpose was harder to define. Elisabeth reminded us it consisted of two aspects, the first being the holding, loving, physical closeness and security that assures children that they are loved and cared for no matter how they look or how they behave, and allowing them to grow up with self-worth and self-respect. The other aspect involves our ability to allow those we love to grow and experience life independently. Elisabeth used the example of the mother tying her son's shoelaces until he was 12. That child, she contended, would always be dependent. We must relinquish our need to do things for those we love as that is a manifestation of lack of faith, not love. Many of us also grow up without uncon-

ditional love, being told in overt or more subtle ways, "I love you IF. . ."
She said these people become prostitutes, bargaining and parceling off
pieces of themselves as they strive to gain external approval. These
people will very often feel a lack of identity as a result: "I don't know who
I am." Devoid of self-worth and self-esteem, they may be great achievers,
but will spend their lives searching in vain for some kind of gratification.

Elisabeth defined loving as never being afraid of the windstorms of
life: "Should you shield the canyon from the windstorms, you would
never see the true beauty of their carvings." These workshops exposed
the participants to these windstorms, so that at the end of their own days,
they would be proud to look in the mirror and be pleased with the
carvings of their own canyons. She added that if we were all raised with
unconditional love, the need for her workshops would disappear. We
would not need that outlet, we would not need to scream out unshed
tears, vent our anger on a mattress. We would not spread our anger,
revenge, hate and self-pity. Instead, we would raise a generation of
healthy children who can grow up with harmony between the physical,
emotional, intellectual and spiritual quadrants.

Four Quadrants

Elisabeth told us that we are each comprised of quadrants which govern
our physical, emotional, intellectual, and spiritual existence. Like our
natural emotions, our successful chronological progression through each
of these quadrants as we mature mentally and physically enables us to
experience life completely.

She asked us to imagine a circle, then divide it down the center and
across the middle into four sections. In the upper right hand corner is the
physical quadrant that we begin to experience at birth until about six
months, the exact ages not being important. The physical quadrant gives
us the tools to experience life by providing sensation. As physical, sensual
beings unable to care for ourselves as infants, we need to be fed, changed,
kept warm and free of harm. If we are not cared for at this stage, right
away we experience a deficit which impedes growth in all succeeding
quadrants, our emotional, intellectual, and spiritual development. The
physical quadrant also functions to give us a sense of our own physical
health, our physical growth, and security — a sense and need for survival. If our physical needs are met and we are not threatened with harm,
we develop a sense of confidence that the world will "take care" of us. If

we are abused or neglected, we are held back from developing through the remaining quadrants by our own fear.

At about six months, Elisabeth continued, we begin to be aware of our emotions through the crying and sadness we feel, for instance, when our parent leaves the room. The focus shifts from our physical needs to our feelings and the development of our emotions. Relationships become important — we define ourselves and others, whether we get along or where we "fit." Our compelling need is to belong, to have a sense of self, to love and be loved. To satisfy that need we begin to express ourselves and our natural emotions — grief, anger, jealousy, fear, and love. If they are repressed or denied, we have feelings of rejection, abandonment, and betrayal which will preclude us from developing intellectually and spiritually. If they are encouraged, when we can express them openly, we develop a sense of self-love and self-esteem.

Around age six, we move into the intellectual quadrant, simply by virtue of the fact that this is the time we typically start going to school. Our development through this quadrant allows us to think creatively and rationally, as well as solve problems. We learn that through the continual development of our intellect comes understanding, a vital prerequisite for survival. If our interactions with our teachers (using the term loosely) are positive, we are affirmed. We learn we have the tools to face any challenges that await us. We are assured that we learn valuable lessons from our mistakes. But sometimes we get ridiculed for those mistakes and we feel wounded and shamed, then stupid and inadequate, even crazy. If, instead, we are encouraged and praised, we have confidence in our intellectual capacity and can be *powerful problem-solvers.*

As we enter the spiritual quadrant at roughly age 13, intuition begins to flower and be available to us. It stimulates growth, a curiosity about one's place within the universe, and a need to explore the existence of a creator. If exploration is denied or a given faith prescribed without room for questioning, we become confused, may experience a lack of fulfillment and identity, and an emptiness. On the other hand, when this quadrant is encouraged and flourishes, we develop a sense of inner peace, that we belong and that life has meaning. We feel connected and with purpose.

Elisabeth explained that our successful development through each quadrant makes us whole. Deficits in earlier quadrants will affect the remaining growth. Her workshops were designed specifically to help people who have these wounds to heal, providing them that safe place to relive and release their pain, rage, and guilt. Shedding our negativity leaves us stronger and more beautiful, she told us, polished like a rock passed through a tumbler. We will reach a state of harmony among the four quadrants, enabling us to truly live in the here and now, to look back in satisfaction, and forward without fear. Once we can accept ourselves, to love and forgive ourselves, then we can learn to do so with others. At this moment, she pointed to the students and said: "Ultimately, it is your choice whether you emerge from the tumbler crushed or polished."

Externalization Workshops

Led by the Staff of the Former Elisabeth Kübler-Ross Center

Lea Adnor is organizing 3-day Life, Loss, and Healing workshops. Lea can be reached at:
> *The Safe Center*
> P.O. Box 611
> Annandale, VA 22003
> *abdnor @ safecenter.com*
> 703–642–8827

Frank Monastero is organizing 3-day Life, Loss, and Transition Workshops. Contact Frank or Jo Ann Thomas at:
> *The Gateway Center*
> 54 Park Avenue
> Bay Shore, NY 11706
> *Gatewayllt@aol.com*
> 516–968–4677

Sharon Tobin leads 5-day Safe Harbors Workshops for abuse and trauma survivors. Sharon can be reached at:
> 2325 West Victory Boulevard
> Burbank, CA 91506

David Mullins organizes The Training Program in Externalization Process (Beginning, Intermediate, and Advanced Levels). For information, contact David at:
> P.O. Box 774
> Willliamsburg, MA 01096
> *DavidMullins@compuserve.com*

Jim Fenley is organizing 3-day Grief, Loss, and Healing Workshops is Asheboro, North Carolina. Jim can be reached at:

Safe Passage
2701 West Market Street
Greensboro, NC 27403
JFenley311@aol.com

Jacob Watson leads a 3-day Grief, Loss, and Compassion Workshop. He can be reached at:

41 Glenwood Avenue
Portland, ME 04103
104136. 2235@compuserve.com

Shep Jeffreys leads Healing Through Loss Workshops in Columbia, Maryland. They are offered at three levels with tracks for the general public and for healthcare professionals. Externalization exercises which do not utilize "mattress work" are included along with didactic and skill building activities. Shep can be reached at:

The Steven Daniel Jeffreys Foundation
jeff23@erols.com

Ralph Stolz is organizing 3-day non-residential Externalization Workshops (And Then They Flew). He can be reached at:

555 Harrison Street
Emmaus, PA 18049
610–867–2320

Jeanette Philips is leading 3-day Externalization Workshops for Couples and a Training Program for Professionals. She can be reached at:

2260 Compass Point Lane
Reston, VA 20191
jphilips@mindspring.com

Larry Lincoln leads 3-day Growth and Transition Workshops. Anne Taylor Lincoln can be contacted at:

2630 N. Santa Lucia
Tucson, AZ 85715
520–325–3100

Roz Leiser, Patricia DeMore, and Robert Gelt organize 3-day Moving through Loss and Transition Workshops in the San Francisco bay area. They can be reached at:

   P.O. Box 31579
   San Francisco, CA 94131
   ROZLEI@aol.com
   GELT@gbn.org

For workshops in the U.K., contact Eolath MaGee at:
   The Fold
   16 Sheepwalk Road
   Stoneyford
   Lisburn
   Co. Antrim BT28 3RB
   Northern Ireland
   011–44–1846–648572

For workshops in France, contact Herve Mignot at:
   EKR France
   60
   Run Michel-Ange
   75016 Paris
   011–33–140–71–6060

For workshops in The Netherlands contact Rochelle Griffin at:
   Vuurvlinder
   Hogestraat 30
   6624 BB
   Haarewaarden
   The Netherlands
   011–31–487–57–3378

For workshops in Spain, contact Alba Payas at:
   Tonar a Casa/Volver a Casa
   Casa Gusta
   17483 Bascara
   Craide Girona 24
   Spain
   tornar@grn.es

For workshops in Israel, contact Shula Keller at:
    Levi Eshkol 445/11
    Ma'alot 21033
    Israel
    011–9724–9977165

For workshops in New Zealand, contact Liese Groot-Alberts at:
    P.O. Box 146
    Oneroa
    Waiheke Island, New Zealand
    011–64–9–630–9507

or Hetty Rodenburg at:
    42 Kotari Road
    Days Bay
    Eastbourne, New Zealand
    011–64–4–562–7475

For workshops in Australia contact Keith Taylor at:
    79 Turpentine Street
    Wyoming 2250
    New South Wales, Australia
    011–61–4–328–4519

Directory of Organizations, Manufacturers and Resources

Barrier-Free Lifts, Inc.
9230 Prince William Street
Manassas, VA 20110
800-582-8732

Best Doctors
1359 Silver Bluff Road
Suite F2
Aken, SC 29803
1-888-DOCTORS
www.bestdoctors.com

Braun Corporation
PO Box 310
Winamac, IN 46996
(800)THE-LIFT
www.braunlift.com

Danmar Products
221 Jackson Industry Drive
Ann Arbor, MI 48103
800-783-1998
danmarpro@aol.com

ELASTIC, Inc.
196 Pheasant Run Road
West Chester, PA 19380
610-436-4801
ecbdmd@ix.netcom.com

Falcon Rehabilitation Service (HiRider wheelchair)
4404 E. 60th Avenue
Commerce City, CO
800-370-6808
www.hirider.com

Latex Allergy News
176 Roosevelt Avenue
Torrington, CT 06790
860-482-6869
debilan@compuserve.com

Maine Anti Gravity Systems
299 Presumpscot Street
Portland, ME 04103
207-781-4570

Mid-Atlantic Mobility
255 E. German School Road
Richmond, VA
800-231-7774

The Myelin Project
Suite 950
1747 Pennsylvania Avenue, NW
Washington, DC 20006
(202) 452-8994

Public Citizen
1600 20th Street, NW
Washington, D.C. 20009
202-588-1000
www.citizen.org

Research America 435
908 King Street, Suite 400E
Alexandria, VA 22314
800-366-2873
www.researchamerica.org

Index